The Company We Keep

America's Endangered Species

Wild beasts and birds are by right not the property merely of people today, but the property of the unborn generations, whose belongings we have no right to squander.

— THEODORE ROOSEVELT

BALD EAGLE Protection afforded by the Endangered Species Act has helped our nation's symbol increase its numbers more than tenfold.

We have seen that the senses and intuitions, the various emotions and faculties ... of which man boasts may be found ... in a well-developed condition in the lower animals.

— CHARLES DARWIN

RED WOLF Captive breeding programs have increased the wolf population from just 17 to over 250.

Our village life would stagnate if it were not for the unexplored forests and meadows that surround it. We need the tonic of wildness ... to wade sometimes in marshes where the bittern and the meadow-hen lurk.

— HENRY DAVID THORE

CALIFORNIA CONDOR Successfully bred in captivity, North America's largest flying bird now struggles to coexist with humans.

Underlying the beauty of the spectacle there is meaning and significance. It is the elusiveness of that meaning that haunts us, that sends us again and again into the natural world where the key to the riddle is hidden.

— RACHEL CARSON

In the relations of man with the animals, with the flowers, with the objects of creation, there is a great ethic, scarcely perceived as yet, which will at length break forth into light.

— VICTOR HUGO

WHOOPING CRANE With only about 320 cranes left, the death of this one from avian cholera represents a serious blow to the species.

The Company We Keep

America's Endangered Species

Douglas H. Chadwick and Joel Sartore

NATIONAL
GEOGRAPHIC
SOCIETY

For my mother, Elise Chadwick, who loves plants, animals, and books. —DC

To everyone, from the field biologists to the editors at the National Geographic Society, who made this book possible. Let's hope it's in time to do some good. —JS

Library of Congress Cataloging-In-Publication Data

Chadwick, Douglas H.
    The company we keep: America's endangered species /
      Douglas Chadwick and Joel Sartore.
        p.   cm.
    Includes index.
    ISBN 0-7922-3310-7
    1. Endangered species—United States.
    2. Endangered species—United States—Pictorial works.
    3. Wildlife conservation—United States.
I. Sartore, Joel. II. National Geographic Society (U.S.) III. Title.
QL84.2.C47 1996
591.52'9'0973—dc20   96-18874
                 CIP

INTRODUCTION

PART ONE

39   What's at stake

PART TWO

75   It's the habitat

PART THREE

105   The company we keep

PART FOUR

145   U.S. Endangered Species List

154   Index

INTRODUCTION

HUMANS ARE ONE OF ABOUT 1.75 MILLION SPECIES that have been identified by science, and many believe that 30 million species or more inhabit this world we call ours. Experts predict that at least one of every four of these life-forms may become extinct by the year 2050, less than a single human lifetime away. It is natural for species to go extinct—but at an average rate of one out of every million per century, based upon the fossil record. The current rate may already be as high as several per day. A biological cataclysm of this magnitude hasn't occurred since the end of the Cretaceous period, when the dinosaurs went under along with many other major groups.

At least 500 species and subspecies of plants and animals have gone extinct in North America since the 1500s; among them, the great auk, the Labrador duck, the heath hen, the Eskimo curlew, the sea mink, Audubon's bighorn sheep, the West Indian monk seal, and the emerald trout. Natural causes appear to have claimed just one of the animals, a marine snail that lived off the coast of New England. We barely got to know many of the others. But we did know the bison, the whooping crane, and the southern trumpeter swan. These animals were part of our heritage and lore, interwoven with our image of a new nation and its grandeur. That they nearly tumbled into oblivion astonished many Americans who believed their country's wildlife bounty was as endless as its frontier.

People today are surprised to hear that in the year 1612 an Englishman killed a bison on the shores of the Potomac River in what is now suburban Washington, D.C. They aren't aware that bison ranged through America's eastern forests during Indian times, while woodland caribou roamed at least as far south as New York and golden grizzlies ambled along the beaches of California. Farther west, bison defined the Great Plains. There were an estimated 60 to 70 million of them, a mass of wool and horn and flesh and thunder that outweighed all the men, women, and children living in the U.S. and Canada today. By the end of the 1800s, fewer than 300 were left in the states. The number of passenger pigeons, which had been in the billions, was fast approaching zero. Elk, pronghorns, roseate spoonbills, Atlantic salmon, and even old-growth Eastern hardwoods were becoming rare.

PLANTS IN PERIL Boldly veined leaves are a trademark of the endangered mahoe, one of 185 Hawaiian plants currently listed as endangered or threatened.

At the turn of the century, with the end of the frontier in plain view, Americans finally paused to take stock. As they did, there were those who found that they cherished what was not yet tamed, and the first stirrings of the American conservation movement were heard. Before long, groups such as the newly formed Audubon Society were lobbying to protect species ravaged by commercial hunting, while citizens sought to set aside some of our public lands as nature reserves.

In 1907, when 15 surviving bison were shipped by train from the Bronx Zoo to reseed a newly established sanctuary in Oklahoma's Wichita Mountains, crowds gathered at each whistlestop, curious, and perhaps a little ashamed, cheering the shaggy beasts onward. More cheering was heard in 1935, when Congress set aside Red Rock Lakes National Wildlife Refuge in Montana's upper Centennial Valley for the sake of the last known trumpeter swans in America.

There were only 73. (At the time, biologists were unaware that other trumpeters had survived in Canada and Alaska.) Southern trumpeters had been found from coast to coast, but they migrated, flying a continental gantlet of shotgun fire twice every year. The largest of the world's waterfowl, borne on wings ten feet across, trumpeter swans were hard to miss, and they were rendered into roasts, pillow stuffing, powder puffs, gloves, and writing quills by the hundreds of thousands.

Red Rock Lakes lies 6,600 feet above sea level, hidden from the outside world by 9,000- and 10,000-foot peaks. The land is snowbound more than half the year, and winter temperatures reach fifty below zero. Yet, as in Yellowstone National Park just to the east, naturally heated springs can be found in the Centennial Valley. A small group of swans could stay here year-round, as could a few swans in the park and on the Henrys Fork of the Snake River in a neighboring portion of Idaho. These were the ones that survived.

May is nesting season for the Red Rock Lakes trumpeters. This high in the Rockies, it is also waterfall time, when snow melts off the peaks in silver cascades and mountain bluebirds perch on newly leafed white aspen in the draws. Pairs of swans fly over their territories in long, low circles, trumpeting past the Centennial Range and the Lima Peaks, past moose with new calves wading along the shores, past the Snowcrest Mountains and antelope grazing the sagebrush foothills, and past the Hilgards, the Sawtells, wandering coyotes, and the distant Madison Range. Without these birds, the observer reflects, the world would go on. But with them, it is still, every now and then, perfect.

With swans having been transplanted from Red Rock Lakes to several other sites in the West, southern trumpeters number almost 3,000 today and appear to be holding their own. The main challenge has been trying to reestablish a migration pattern for the new groups that keeps the area from becoming overcrowded and allows for an ample food supply once winter sets in.

In 1937, about the same time Red Rock Lakes was made a reserve, Congress established Aransas National Wildlife Refuge on the Texas coast to safeguard the main wintering ground for whooping cranes, the tallest birds on the continent. No more than a dozen or so breeding pairs remained. Unlike the last remaining swans, whooping cranes continued to migrate each year, nesting in Wood Buffalo National Park in Canada's Northwest Territories. It is a long and risky trip, one reason the birds have increased very slowly despite decades of special protection, captive breeding, and attempts to develop an alternate population by placing some whooper young with sandhill crane foster parents. The effort has yielded a current population of more than 300.

Many other wildlife refuges and national parks were set aside as havens in the early part of the century as the federal government assumed a larger role in protecting natural resources. Conservation groups continued to gain members. Game laws and the emerging field of wildlife management encouraged the protection of hunted animals. Yet all kinds of species lumped together as "non-game" were falling through this loosely woven safety net, particularly big carnivores. Practically everyone continued to persecute them. Even park officials and wildlife managers took part, believing that their mission was to rid nature of "undesirable" animals and look after the "useful" ones. As the human population soared, land use turned more intensive and industry more pervasive, and a broader array of species went into decline. Yet with many game populations flourishing due to strong financial and political support from sportsmen, the public was only vaguely aware of the problems building for wildlife in general.

By the middle of the 20th century, it was getting harder to deny that something was seriously amiss in the wildlife kingdom. The grandest carnivore in the lower 48 states, the grizzly bear, was reduced to fewer than 1,000 as chain saws and bulldozers chewed away at the last backcountry strongholds in the Rockies. The biggest creatures that ever took breath, the great whales, looked to be headed the way of the dodo. Though they had all the world's seven seas to roam, there was not enough room to escape modern whaling technology. The country's biggest reptiles, the American alligator and American crocodile, were being poached out of existence in what had long been portrayed as impenetrable swamps. The peregrine falcon, able to dive at speeds in excess of 150 miles per hour, was rarely seen in the U.S. any more. Even America's national symbol, the bald eagle, was in a tailspin and in danger of disappearing from the lower 48 states, though it had been protected from shooting since 1940.

Worries about atomic fallout had sensitized the public to the possible danger of invisible contaminants, and to the fact that we were now capable of exterminating even ourselves. Soon the metabolism-warping pesticide DDT stood accused of killing countless songbirds like the bluebird and robin, leaving backyard gardens silent. When the decline of the peregrine falcon, bald eagle, and other raptors was linked to eggshell-thinning caused by the same chemical, people suddenly grew alarmed. They started to ask themselves whether other pesticides, herbicides, and industrial pollutants would turn out to be toxic.

While concerns about the health effects of pollution were growing, tremendous advances were being made in our understanding of biological systems, especially in two relatively new fields. One was molecular biology; James Watson and Francis Crick had just cracked the code for DNA in 1953. The other was ecology, focusing on the interconnections between different organisms and between living communities and their environment. The word itself was just beginning to work its way into everyday usage when a set of pictures arrived from space. Taken by some of the first American astronauts, the photos captured a cloud-tressed blue sphere shining alone in the black void. Spaceship Earth. The images transformed human consciousness. Our understanding of where we live would never be the same again. It became all too clear that if we were to ruin the life-support system on this one-of-a-kind vessel, there would be no hope of rescue.

The 1960s ushered in a sustained effort to try and make things right in the natural world. The era saw passage of the 1963 Clean Air Act, 1964 Wilderness Act, 1969 National Environmental Policy Act, and the first Earth Day in 1970. In 1972, responding to the warnings of scientists and a growing concern for wildlife among voters, Congress approved new federal water pollution controls, the Marine Mammal Protection Act, the Coastal Zone Management Act, and the Federal Environmental Pesticide Control Act, which curtailed the use of DDT and other chlorinated hydrocarbons and led to a ban on certain poisons in widespread use. This unprecedented burst of environmental awareness culminated with the much-praised, much-scorned Endangered Species Act (ESA) of 1973.

CONGRESS RECOGNIZED SPECIES LOSS as an issue of national concern as early as 1900, when it passed the Lacey Act, making it illegal to import foreign creatures without a permit or to transport unlawfully killed wildlife across state boundaries. With the signing of a "Seal Treaty" in 1911, the U.S., Great Britain, Japan, and Russia agreed to control the harvest that threatened to wipe out fur seals and sea otters. In 1916, the U.S. and Great Britain, representing Canada, ratified a treaty protecting many of the game birds that migrate between the two North American countries. Congress followed up with the 1918 Federal Migratory Bird Treaty Act, broadening federal powers to regulate the harvest of bird species.

Almost another half century would go by before any comprehensive legislation was proposed to deal with vanishing wildlife. The first attempt was the Endangered Species Preservation Act of 1966, sparked by a report from the Department of Interior naming 83 species of vertebrates at risk of disappearing, including the blue whale, the grizzly, the black-footed ferret, the California condor, the tule white-fronted goose, and the Kauai `o`o of Hawaii. This act directed the Interior Secretary to create an official federal list of imperiled native animals and to take steps to bolster their survival. Providing no enforcement powers and few funds for recovery work, the bill was largely symbolic. But it was a start.

Congress tried again three years later. The 1969 Endangered Species Conservation Act expanded the Lacey Act's ban on interstate commerce to embrace reptiles, amphibians, mollusks, and crustaceans. The inclusion of reptiles was mainly intended to curtail rampant alligator poaching. Although adding mollusks and crustaceans may not have seemed too dramatic, it was the first time that the welfare of invertebrates had been addressed. Just ahead waited a new era of conservation based upon a greater appreciation of species's roles in the natural balance of biological systems.

The 1969 act required the Interior Secretary to maintain the list of U.S. species in danger and to draw up a parallel list of species "threatened with worldwide extinction," and called for a global conference to address the problem. This led in 1973 to the Convention on International Trade in Endangered Species (CITES), which established trade restrictions to protect vanishing wildlife.

One of the main concerns at the time was the assault on the world's various wild cats. Coats made from their fur were in great demand, a stylish symbol of disposable wealth. Cheetahs, clouded leopards, and North America's lynx were among the sources of this finery being wiped out—just like the swans, whooping cranes, egrets, terns, and now extinct Carolina parakeets whose plumage fed the American fashion industry of the previous century. Before long, CITES would turn its attention to products made from sea turtles and to the flourishing and highly destructive trade in exotic pet birds.

During the late 1980s, prices for elephant tusks reached a point where they were worth more than their weight in silver. The mad scramble for ivory was destabilizing governments through corruption and the incursions of foreign poaching gangs, and it was leaving the tropics littered with colossal, grey carcasses. Earth's largest land mammals were falling at a rate of more than 2,000 per week. CITES's 1990 ban on the import of ivory effectively, if belatedly, brought the mayhem to a halt. The importance of this organization grows by the year, for as a source of illegal profits around the globe, wildlife is now exceeded only by drugs.

On the domestic front, the 1969 act proved far less effective. Once again, enforcement powers were vague and funds inadequate. The question of where traditional state control over wildlife ended and federal jurisdiction began was not adequately resolved. Though many of the species at risk had high public profiles, recovering them—as opposed to merely listing them—seemed a low priority within the government itself. As of 1971, the U.S. Fish and Wildlife Service, the branch of the Interior Department responsible for most endangered species work, had two biologists and one secretary assigned to manage the entire program. Not a single native species was added to its endangered list between December 1970 and June 1973, though plenty of them qualified.

BASED ON THE ASSUMPTIONS that each life-form may prove valuable in ways we cannot yet measure and that each is entitled to exist for its own sake as well, the Endangered Species Act of 1973 amounted to nothing less than a rudimentary bill of rights for wildlife—an attempt to guarantee a future for as many species as possible, even if doing so required real sacrifice on our part. Confronting the tide of extinction head-on, the landmark bill clearly laid out what was at stake:

"The Congress finds and declares that:

(1) various species of fish, wildlife, and plants in the United States have been rendered extinct as a consequence of economic growth and development untempered by adequate concern and conservation;

(2) other species of fish, wildlife, and plants have been so depleted in numbers that they are in danger of, or threatened with, extinction;

(3) these species of fish, wildlife, and plants are of esthetic, ecological, educational, historical, recreational, and scientific value to the Nation and its people;

(4) the United States has pledged itself as a sovereign state in the international community to conserve to the extent practicable the various species of fish or wildlife and plants facing extinction...." (*from the ESA*)

Earlier protection efforts not only had focused mainly on vertebrates but also had been directed chiefly at the two warm-blooded classes: birds, perhaps the most visible wildlife in our everyday lives and the group with the keenest following among nature enthusiasts, and our fellow mammals. The 1973 bill redefined fish and wildlife to include invertebrates, which make up more than 90 percent of U.S. fauna, extending the safety net to catch any member of the animal kingdom other than insects ruled to be pests.

Plants, which make up about 18 percent of America's species and form the very foundation of wildlife communities, were also made eligible for the first time. Such policies set the stage for modern conservation biology, whose goal is to safeguard biological diversity—defined as the full array of native species and all the processes and interactions that sustain them.

The ESA went on to establish and identify two distinct categories for species in peril: "endangered" referred to species in immediate danger of extinction—those with three toes over the brink. The second status, "threatened," applied to "any species which is likely to become an endangered species within the forseeable future throughout all or a significant portion of its range." The point was to identify creatures starting to slip toward the abyss and get to work solving their troubles before things reached the critical stage.

To insulate the species selection process from the political influence wielded by various interest groups, the decision to list a plant or animal was to be based solely on the best scientific data available, independent of any economic considerations. Whether or not an organism was threatened or endangered was a matter of its numbers, the size and condition of its habitat, and the threats to its survival. Period.

The ESA would be administered primarily by the Fish and Wildlife Service. Where marine species of economic value were involved—salmon, for example—part of the responsibility shifted to the National Marine Fisheries Service, a branch of the Commerce Department.

Section 7 of the act required all federal agencies to undertake programs to conserve listed species. No federal agency could proceed with any action that might put a listed species at risk or destroy or alter its critical habitat. Fully one-third of the U.S. is federal domain, and that acreage contains roughly half the ranges currently occupied by listed species. Considering as well the number of public works undertaken by federal agencies, from the Federal Highway Administration to the Corps of Engineers, the scope of Section 7 is astonishing. In much the same way that the inclusion of invertebrates and plants as wildlife heralded the new emphasis on biological diversity, Section 7's call for interagency consultation made it possible to practice natural resource planning on a larger, more meaningful scale—at the level of landscapes and watersheds—and ecosystem management would become an official federal policy under the Clinton administration.

Section 9 of the ESA outlawed the buying, selling, or transporting of listed species. Most important, it prohibited taking them in the first place. To "take" was defined as "to harass, harm, pursue, hunt, shoot, wound, kill, trap, capture, or collect, or to attempt to engage in any such conduct." Violators were subject to serious fines. Moreover, the taking of imperiled species was prohibited on private land as well as on public domain.

Balancing the powers of government with the rights of private citizens is fundamental to a republic, and the concept of being prohibited from "taking" an endangered species on private land was new and unsettling. It had never been clear who, if anyone, really owned the wildlife on private property. People started to worry about the federal government deeming their property off limits to various activities for the sake of some creature hardly anyone else knew or cared was there. Real estate developers and industry advocates had their own complaints about the act's jurisdiction over private ground and eagerly joined small landholders in what became known as the property rights movement. The "taking" that its supporters worried about was not of species but of citizens' freedom to do as they pleased with their land, a privilege long taken for granted and jealously guarded. Some warned that, rather than face possible federal restrictions, they would plow meadows or cut down woods to rid them of endangered species, and a few carried out their threat.

Ranchers, loggers, miners, oil and gas operators, and others who had enjoyed ready access to raw materials on federal domain were unhappy with the growing body of new environmental regulations affecting them. The ESA seemed to snatch away what little wriggle room they had left. "We're the ones that are endangered," insisted spokesmen for natural resource industries. More resistance arose from desert motorcycle racers, beach buggy enthusiasts, powerboaters, rare plant hobbyists, reptile collectors, land speculators, commercial fishermen, trappers. There came to be almost as many kinds of objections to the act as there were groups running up against new constraints on their activities.

Over the years, the opposition gathered political momentum, and a number of anti-ESA measures have recently been sponsored in Congress. Some seek to weaken the act's jurisdiction over both private lands and commercial activities on public lands. Others would redefine "taking" so that as long as you don't directly harm an imperiled creature, you can do whatever you like to its habitat. Still others propose making economic considerations part of the criteria for listing.

Annual funding for the endangered species program from 1973 through 1990 averaged 39 million dollars, or about 16 cents a year per taxpayer. The budget briefly rose to about 70 million per year but then was cut back to 60 million for fiscal year 1996. Some consider that sum a waste of taxpayers' hard-earned money. Others call it paltry and inadequate for ensuring the survival of America's biological heritage; the Pentagon, they note, annually loses almost half that amount on one hotel it leases in Orlando, Florida. Funding for research on manatees, opposed by the power boating industry, may be cut in half if current proposals before Congress are passed, and conservationists warn that the Endangered Species Act itself is endangered.

Polls consistently show that at least two-thirds of the public support the ESA, and a majority say they would be willing to pay more to protect wildlife. That does not necessarily mean people favor every organism sheltered by the act, though. Other polls show support for endangered species dropping off rather quickly as you move from large, lovely, or cuddly creatures to the likes of bugs, slugs, and plants with names like white bladderpod and ashy dogweed. True, the current ESA budget wouldn't build one mile of urban interstate highway, but there are other costs to society in the form of business delayed or foregone. Many extra dollars and hours are now spent complying with regulations and plodding through a more cautious planning process.

Does it make sense to fuss over each and every one of those so-called "lower" life-forms that many perceive to be of little value, if not downright worthless? Should we restrict development to save the endangered Socorro isopod, a primitive organism in the group commonly called pillbugs, when there are other isopod species practically everywhere you look? And what of species whose critical habitat spans an enormous area? Are we willing to revise timber and hydropower projects throughout the Pacific Northwest in order to salvage an endangered salmon species when you can buy canned salmon at any supermarket?

Arguments over the ESA are not likely to end any time soon. The basic problem of species loss certainly won't, not with so many of us competing with native plants and animals and each other for the same amount of room. In 1790, the U.S. population stood at just under 4 million. By 1890, it was about 63 million, almost a

16-fold increase. As of 1990, the U.S. had nearly 250 million human inhabitants. In 2050, more than 400 million are expected. We are home to the third-largest population on the globe after China and India and, between births and immigration, have the highest rate of increase among wealthy nations.

There were 109 names on the 1973 list of endangered and threatened species. The current total is more than 950—more than 1,500 when counting foreign species. Among states, Hawaii has the most listed species, with more than 220. Each island supports a unique set of tropical flora and fauna, and island ecosystems tend to be much more vulnerable to disruption than those on the mainland. California is second, with more than 160 listed species, reflecting its rank as the most populous state. Florida, our fourth most populous state, is third, with more than 90 listed species. On the opposite end of the scale is Alaska. It has the lowest density of humans, the most intact ecosystems, and the fewest listed species—five at last count.

Waiting in line behind the listed species are nearly 4,000 officially recognized candidates, which may qualify for ESA protection but have not yet undergone a full review. The bottleneck has been the shortage of money for ESA work. In August 1995 the review process shut down altogether as Congress placed a moratorium on new listings pending reauthorization of the act. Fights over proposals to weaken the ESA were so bitter and polarized that Congress renewed the moratorium in March 1996 while putting off reauthorization yet again. In May, President Clinton lifted the ban, allowing the Fish and Wildlife Service to begin addressing a backlog of 243 species that had been awaiting final listing decisions. The money allocated specifically for listing was cut from 6 million to 4 million for fiscal year 1996, and the Fish and Wildlife Service faced hundreds of notices of intent to sue if it proceeded with plans to protect the plants and animals in question. Nevertheless, on May 20 the agency announced that it was back in business by granting threatened status to the California red-legged frog, largest of the native frogs in the western United States and the inspiration for Mark Twain's short story, "The Celebrated Jumping Frog of Calaveras County."

The National Biological Service has identified 126 "imperiled areas" in the U.S. Located mainly in the East, these are endangered ecosystems, which have lost more than 70 percent of their natural habitats. Between 90 and 95 percent of the virgin forests in the lower 48 states have been eliminated, as have 97 percent of Connecticut's undeveloped shorelines, virtually all of Kentucky's native prairies, 88 percent of Florida's slash pine forests, and 99 percent of California's native grasslands, to list but a few examples. They promise a cascade of more threatened and endangered wildlife, whether anyone is still listing species or not.

Remarkably, the ESA faced little opposition when the bill was introduced. Congress passed it unanimously. Amendments, however, have altered the act in the intervening years. One revision allows economic factors to be taken into consideration when defining critical habitat for listed species. Another gives less protection to endangered species reintroduced to an area as "experimental" populations. A third adds prohibitions against collecting or destroying listed plants.

More adjustments will surely be made over time. Environmentalists themselves are suggesting ways to provide incentives for encouraging private landowners to protect species on their property, and to match federal guidelines more closely to the needs of local human communities. Secretary of the Interior Bruce Babbitt recently went a step further and exempted most small landholders from restrictions against taking endangered species.

The tricky part about modifying the ESA is that its uncompromising qualities are precisely what made it a catalyst for change. There are no compromises about extinction itself. It is a one-way passage into nothingness. Once gone, a particular organism, with its unique chemistry and code of genetic instructions for how to live on the planet, whatever splendor of form and behavior it might have offered, will be gone forever.

GIVEN THE MAGNITUDE OF WHAT THE ESA SET OUT TO ACCOMPLISH, it would have been surprising if the law got everything exactly right the first time around. But most would agree that it got some important things right. We cannot help seeing ourselves in other life-forms. We share too many qualities to ignore, beginning with the miracle of our existence. For the same reason, we can't help but feel a powerful sense of loss when another species vanishes. Suddenly, our planet seems a bit more lonely and our underpinnings a little less solid. The desire to save endangered species is both evidence of our extraordinary capacity for empathy and an expression of common sense in regard to our own long-term survival.

In the early 1960s only about 400 breeding pairs of bald eagles were left in the lower 48 states. At the moment, the count is estimated to be over 5,000. By June 1994 the status of our national symbol was sufficiently improved in most places to be upgraded from endangered to threatened. The species may be declared recovered and taken off the list altogether before long.

Because the eagle's plight helped spur both the eventual ban on DDT and passage of the 1973 act, other species that chip their way out of eggs to trace signatures of freedom across American skies have largely recovered as well. Peregrine falcons have rebounded from fewer than 50 pairs in 1975 to more than 1,300 pairs today. Brown pelicans and ospreys are becoming common again. Bluebirds and their songs have returned to our yards.

We now pay much closer attention to the chemicals in our environment. We take more seriously the evidence that the same ecosystems these creatures depend upon ultimately sustain humankind. And we've known all along that nature replenishes the human spirit as well. Future generations may look back and decide that while we were trying to save the bald eagle, what really happened is that the eagle—and the manatee and the prairie fringed orchid—saved us.

ENDANGERED IN PARADISE The nene, Hawaii's state bird, once roamed across much of the island chain. Now it is restricted to the highlands of Hawaii and Maui. Though hunting triggered the bird's decline in the 18th and 19th centuries, current threats are a shrinking habitat, a shortage of native food plants, and predation from introduced species like the mongoose. Hope for the species rests with captive breeding programs, which have boosted the population from a low of about 30 in 1952 to several hundred today.

America's Endangered Species

The following pages list, according to primary threat, every endangered species in America and its waters. Whether the threat was created accidentally—like the introduction of mosquitoes to Hawaii—or deliberately—like the clearing of vast forests—each is the result of human activity. Starting with 109 plants and animals in 1973, the Endangered Species Act now protects more than 1,500 species, from whales to flies. Though not always popular, the ESA has done a remarkable job of preserving America's spectacular diversity of life.

HABITAT LOSS

northern aplomado falcon
Falco femoralis septentrionalis

Habitat loss is by far the largest threat facing America's endangered species. In the case of the Northern aplomado falcon, the loss of grasslands throughout the Southwest has nearly eliminated the bird from America. In the Southeast, dams have flooded the fast-moving streams inhabited by mussels; as a result, 56 mussel species are endangered or threatened, and over 20 may already be gone. But the threats to a habitat are often more subtle than a dam. The use of the pesticide DDT, for example, invisibly poisoned entire ecosystems, moving up the food chain until it nearly destroyed the bald eagle and brown pelican.

koki'o
Kokia drynarioides

green-blossom pearlymussel
Epioblasma torulosa gubernaculum

crested honeycreeper
Palmeria dolei

Karner blue butterfly
Lycaeides melissa samuelis

Lakela's mint
Dicerandra immaculata

`akiapola`au
Hemignathus munroi

Lewton's polygala
Polygala lewtonii

Kretschmarr Cave mold beetle
Texamaurops reddelli

Roanoke logperch
Percina rex

Garrett's mint
Dicerandra christmanii

shortnose sturgeon
Acipenser brevirostrum

Sonoma spineflower
Chorizanthe valida

San Diego button-celery
Eryngium aristulatum var. parishii

Attwater's greater prairie-chicken
Tympanuchus cupido attwateri

Maryland darter
Etheostoma sellare

marsh sandwort
Arenaria paludicola

pink mucket pearlymussel
Lampsilis abrupta

Colorado squawfish
Ptychocheilus lucius

Gambel's watercress
Rorippa gambellii

giant kangaroo rat
Dipodomys ingens

humpback chub
Gila cypha

black-capped vireo
Vireo atricapillus

dark pigtoe
Pleurobema furvum

Devils Hole pupfish
Cyprinodon diabolis

Otay mesa mint
Pogogyne nudiuscula

sandlace
Polygonella myriophylla

clubshell
Pleurobema clava

lesser long-nosed bat
Leptonycteris curasoae yerbabuenae

Bradshaw's desert-parsley
Lomatium bradshawii

Delhi Sands flower-loving fly
Rhaphiomidas terminatus abdominalis

Molokai thrush
Myadestes lanaiensis rutha

tulotoma snail
Tulotoma magnifica

Hawaii creeper
Oreomystis mana

Amargosa niterwort
Nitrophila mohavensis

American crocodile
Crocodylus acutus

wood stork
Mycteria americana

Applegate's milk-vetch
Astragalus applegatei

Lost River sucker
Deltistes luxatus

Mississippi sandhill crane
Grus canadensis pulla

bluemask darter
Etheostoma (Doration) n. sp.

Barneby reed-mustard
Schoenocrambe barnebyi

running buffalo clover
Trifolium stoloniferum

blunt-nosed leopard lizard
Gambelia silus

American chaffseed
Schwalbea americana

Arizona cliffrose
Purshia subintegra

Palezone shiner
Notropis n. sp.

Menzies' wallflower
Erysimum menziesii

beach layia
Layia carnosa

Plymouth redbelly turtle
Pseudemys rubriventris bangsi

Chamaesyce halemanui

Florida perforate cladonia / *Cladonia perforata*

beach jacquemontia / *Jacquemontia reclinata*

desert slender salamander / *Batrachoseps aridus*

Apalachicola rosemary / *Conradina glabra*

Texas blind salamander / *Typhlomolge rathbuni*

little Aguja pondweed / *Potamogeton clystocarpus*

Oahu tree snails / *Achatinella spp.*

Antioch Dunes evening-primrose / *Oenothera deltoides ssp. howellii*

deltoid spurge / *Chamaesyce deltoidea ssp. deltoidea*

Schiedea haleakalensis

Alabama canebrake pitcher-plant / *Sarracenia rubra ssp. alabamensis*

 appalachian monkeyface pearlymussel / *Quadrula sparsa*

Alabama leather flower / *Clematis socialis*

mat-forming quillwort / *Isoetes tegetiformans*

mission blue butterfly / *Icaricia icarioides missionensis*

Virginia big-eared bat / *Plecotus townsendii virginianus*

snakeroot / *Eryngium cuneifolium*

Ash Meadows speckled dace / *Rhinichthys osculus nevadensis*

Pahranagat roundtail chub / *Gila robusta jordani*

Indiana bat / *Myotis sodalis*

flat pigtoe / *Pleurobema marshalli*

Diamond Head schiedea / *Schiedea adamantis*

Cumberland monkeyface pearlymussel / *Quadrula intermedia*

 nerican burying beetle / *Nicrophorus americanus*

Hawaiian hawk / *Buteo solitarius*

Nashville crayfish / *Orconectes shoupi*

Small's milkpea / *Galactia smallii*

`o`u / *Psittirostra psittacea*

fat pocketbook / *Potamilus capax*

clover lupine / *Lupinus tidestromii*

amber darter / *Percina antesella*

Maui parrotbill / *Pseudonestor xanthophrys*

na`u / *Gardenia brighamii*

woodland caribou / *Rangifer tarandus caribou*

nukupu`u / *Hemignathus lucidus*

 North Park phacelia / *Phacelia formosula*

Snake River physa snail / *Physa natricina*

Howell's spineflower / *Chorizanthe howellii*

whooping crane / *Grus americana*

Robbins' cinquefoil / *Potentilla robbinsiana*

triangular kidneyshell / *Ptychobranchus greeni*

California Orcutt grass / *Orcuttia californica*

 ovate clubshell / *Pleurobema perovatum*

 red-cockaded woodpecker / *Picoides borealis*

Tennessee yellow-eyed grass / *Xyris tennesseensis*

 San Diego mesa mint / *Pogogyne abramsii*

 black-footed ferret / *Mustela nigripes*

 fine-rayed pigtoe / *Fusconaia cuneolus*

Hawaiian stilt / *Himantopus mexicanus knudseni*

woundfin / *Plagopterus argentissimus*

Cape Sable seaside sparrow / *Ammodramus maritimus mirabilis*

Sonoran pronghorn / *Antilocapra americana sonoriensis*

Comanche Springs pupfish / *Cyprinodon elegans*

`ohe`ohe / *Tetraplasandra gymnocarpa*

 Hay's Spring amphipod / *Stygobromus hayi*

 Key Largo cotton mouse / *Peromyscus gossypinus allapaticola*

Ko`oko`olau / *Bidens micrantha ssp. kalealaha*

northern riffleshell / *Epioblasma torulosa rangiana*

 Monterey gilia / *Gilia tenuiflora ssp. arenaria*

 Gahnia lanaiensis

dromedary pearlymussel / *Dromus dromas*

po`ouli / *Melamprosops phaeosoma*

Florida torreya / *Torreya taxifolia*

light-footed clapper rail / *Rallus longirostris levipes*

Butte County meadowfoam / *Limnanthes floccosa ssp. californica*

Cooley's meadowrue / *Thalictrum cooleyi*

 southern combshell / *Epioblasma penita*

Lower Keys rabbit / *Sylvilagus palustris hefneri*

Ko`oko`olau / *Bidens wiebkei*

Cahaba shiner / *Notropis cahabae*

Virginia fringed mountain snail / *Polygyriscus virginianus*

 ungerford's crawling water beetle / *Brychius hungerfordi*

 southern acornshell / *Epioblasma othcaloogensis*

harperella / *Ptilimnium nodosum*

 white wartyback pearlymussel / *Plethobasus cicatricosus*

 scrub plum / *Prunus geniculata*

 southern clubshell / *Pleurobema decisum*

 Peebles Navajo cactus / *Pediocactus peeblesianus var. peeblesianus*

 Bone Cave harvestman / *Texella reyesi*

Carter's panicgrass / *Panicum fauriei var. carteri*

furbish lousewort / *Pedicularis furbishiae*

`Ewa Plains `akoko / *Chamaesyce skottsbergii var. kalaeloana*

 Penland beardtongue / *Penstemon penlandii*

 San Francisco
garter snake
*Thamnophis sirtalis
tetrataenia*

Hawaiian bluegrass
Poa sandvicensis

Alabama redbelly turtle
Pseudemys alabamensis

Rugel's pawpaw
Deeringothamnus rugelii

Houston toad
Bufo houstonensis

Columbian white-
tailed deer
*Odocoileus virginianus
leucurus*

shiny pigtoe
Fusconaia cor

tidewater goby
Eucyclogobius newberryi

Short's goldenrod
Solidago shortii

heavy pigtoe
Pleurobema taitianum

Avon Park harebells
Crotalaria avonensis

white
…nianus

 June sucker
Chasmistes liorus

wireweed
Polygonella basiramia

Riverside fairy shrimp
Streptocephalus woottoni

Banbury Springs
limpet
Lanx n. sp.

clay phacelia
Phacelia argillacea

Clear Creek gambusia
Gambusia heterochir

Ruth's golden aster
Pityopsis ruthii

Coffin Cave mold beetle
Batrisodes texanus

Idaho springsnail
Fontelicella idahoensis

San Joaquin kit fox
Vulpes macrotis mutica

Carter's mustard
Warea carteri

's-beak
…imus ssp

 black-spored quillwort
Isoetes melanospora

birdwing pearlymussel
Conradilla caelata

four-petal pawpaw
Asimina tetramera

*Delissea
rhytidosperma*

pedate checker-mallow
Sidalcea pedata

shortnose sucker
Chasmistes brevirostris

tan riffleshell
Epioblasma walkeri

Kodachrome
bladderpod
Lesquerella tumulosa

watercress darter
Etheostoma nuchale

Ben Lomond wallflower
Erysimum teretifolium

fanshell
Cyprogenia stegaria

…flowe
…reinitzii

 Ben Lomond
spineflower
*Chorizanthe pungens var.
hartwegiana*

beautiful pawpaw
*Deeringothamnus
pulchellus*

Bruneau Hot springsnail
Pyrgulopsis bruneauensis

*Schiedea
kaalae*

Michaux's sumac
Rhus michauxii

purple cat's paw
pearlymussel
*Epioblasma obliquata
obliquata*

pygmy madtom
Noturus stanauli

longspurred mint
Dicerandra cornutissima

black lace cactus
*Echinocereus reichenbachii
var. albertii*

unarmored threespine
stickleback
*Gasterosteus aculeatus
williamsoni*

Eureka dune grass
Swallenia alexandrae

…lies'-
…rksii

 Virgin River chub
Gila robusta semidnuda

wide-leaf warea
Warea amplexifolia

Myrtle's silverspot
butterfly
Speyeria zerene myrtleae

Pecos gambusia
Gambusia nobilis

razorback sucker
Xyrauchen texanus

robust spineflower
Chorizanthe robusta

Hawaiian goose
Nesochen sandvicensis

little-wing pearlymussel
Pegias fabula

Gila trout
Oncorhynchus gilae

winged mapleleaf
mussel
Quadrula fragosa

palila
Loxioides bailleui

…oot
…a alai

 Gila topminnow
Poeciliopsis occidentalis

El Segundo blue
butterfly
Euphilotes battoides allyni

Cumberland pigtoe
Pleurobema gibberum

autumn buttercup
*Ranunculus acriformis
var. aestivalis*

Modoc sucker
Catostomus microps

Eureka Valley
evening-primrose
*Oenothera avita ssp.
eurekensis*

Coosa moccasinshell
Medionidus parvulus

Kendall Warm Springs
dace
Rhinichthys osculus

orange-foot pimpleback
pearlymussel
Plethobasus cooperianus

Saint Francis' satyr
butterfly
*Neonympha mitchellii
francisci*

green pitcher-plant
Sarracenia oreophila

…eper
…mmea

 bunched arrowhead
Sagittaria fasciculata

West Indian manatee
Trichechus manatus

Higgins' eye
pearlymussel
Lampsilis higginsi

Walker's manioc
Manihot walkerae

cracking pearlymussel
Hemistena lata

desert pupfish
Cyprinodon macularius

Alabama beach mouse
*Peromyscus polionotus
ammobates*

blowout penstemon
Penstemon haydenii

Smoky madtom
Noturus baileyi

San Joaquin
wooly-threads
Lembertia congdonii

jaguarundi
*Felis yagouaroundi
cacomitli*

…each
…ionotu…

Asplenium fragile var. insulare

mehamehame
Flueggea neowawraea

Remya kauaiensis

Hesperomannia arbuscula

Remya montgomeryi

`oha wai
Clermontia oblongifolia ssp. brevipes

Dubautia pauciflorula

San Clemente Island Indian paintbrush
Castilleja grisea

Gouania vitifolia

aupaka
Isodendrion hosakae

na`ena`e
Dubautia herbstobatae

dwarf iliau
Wilkesia hobdyi

ha`iwale
Cyrtandra crenata

Lipochaeta venosa

holei
Ochrosia kilaueaensis

laukahi kuahiwi
Plantago hawaiensis

Diellia pallida

haha
Cyanea procera

haha
Cyanea stictophylla

haha
Cyanea shipmannii

haha
Cyanea mceldowneyi

`oha wai
Clermontia lindseyana

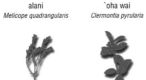

haha
Cyanea hamatiflora ssp. carlsonii

`akoko
Chamaesyce deppeana

loulu
Pritchardia affinic

ha`iwale
Lycopodium nutans

San Clemente Island larkspur
Delphinium variegatum ssp. kinkiense

`awikiwiki
Canavalia molokaiensis

Tetramolopium arenarium

Hawaiian red-flowered geranium
Geranium arboreum

ha`iwale
Cyrtandra tintinnabula

Mariscus fauriei

loulu
Pritchardia munroi

Texas snowbells
Styrax texana

alani
Melicope pallida

alani
Melicope quadrangularis

`oha wai
Clermontia pyrularia

opuhe
Urera kaalae

alani
Melicope lydgatei

haha
Cyanea pinnatifida

Sanicula mariversa

haha
Cyanea mannii

Tetramolopium filiforme

Lobelia niihauensis

alani
Melicope knudsenii

Hesperomannia arborescens

Silene alexandri

nioi
Eugenia koolauensis

ha`iwale
Cyrtandra giffardii

nehe
Lipochaeta tenuifolia

Silene lanceolata

`olulu
Brighamia insignis

`ahinahina
Argyroxiphium sandwicense ssp. sandwicense

kulu`i
Nototrichium humile

Phyllostegia mannii

nehe
Lipochaeta fauriei

`awiwi
Centaurium sebaeoides

`oha wai
Clermontia oblongifolia ssp. mauiensis

Munroidendron racemosum

pamakani
Viola chamissoniana ssp. chamissoniana

haha
Cyanea truncata

wawa`iole
Huperzia mannii

Stenogyne angustifolia var. angustifolia

Stenogyne campanulata

Na Pali beach hedyotis
Hedyotis st.-johnii

Poa siphonoglossa

Rollandia crispa

Neraudia angulata

Santa Barbara Island liveforever
Dudleya traskiae

San Clemente Island bush-mallow
Malacothamnus clementinus

Dubautia latifolia

Lobelia oahuensis

Hawaiian dark-rumped petrel
Pterodroma phaeopygia sandwichensis

Hawaiian monk seal
Monachus schauinslandi

Hawaiian hoary bat
Lasiurus cinereus semotus

piping plover
Charadrius melodus

Schiedea lydgatei

white irisette
Sisyrinchium dichotomum

Mancos milk-vetch
Astragalus humillimus

peregrine falcon
Falco peregrinus

Laysan duck
Anas laysanensis

Virginia northern flying squirrel
Glaucomys sabrinus fuscus

Tar River spinymussel
Elliptio steinstansana

Cushenbury oxytheca
Oxytheca parishii var. goodmaniana

white-rayed pentachaeta
Pentachaeta bellidiflora

Indian Knob mountain balm
Eriodictyon altissimum

vernal pool tadpole shrimp
Lepidurus packardi

`ohai
Sesbania tomentosa

Vigna o-wahuensis

alani
Melicope balloui

white sturgeon
Acipenser transmontanus

Hine's emerald dragonfly
Somatochlora hineana

PREDATION

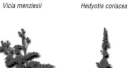

po`e
Portulaca sclerocarpa

Hawaiian plants, like the po`e, dominate this category. Eaten, uprooted, and trampled by feral goats and pigs, these species have few defenses and in many cases have dwindled to dangerously low numbers. Hawaiian officials are trying to control the wild animal population; the survival of many species depends on how well they succeed.

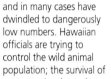

Stenogyne bifida

alani
Melicope haupuensis

haha
Cyanea grimesiana ssp. obatae

liliwai
Acaena exigua

`aiea
Nothocestrum breviflorum

koki`o ke`oke`o
Hibiscus arnottianus ssp. immaculatus

pua `ala
Brighamia rockii

Lysimachia filifolia

haha
Cyanea asarifolia

a`e
Zanthoxylum hawaiiense

wahine noho kula
Isodendrion pyrifolium

heau
Exocarpos luteolus

Clay's hibiscus
Hibiscus clayi

`awiwi
Hedyotis cookiana

Schiedea spergulina var. leiopoda

nohoanu
Geranium multiflorum

`ahinahina
Argyroxiphium sandwicense ssp. macrocephalum

Gouania hillebrandii

`oha wai
Clermontia peleana

nehe
Lipochaeta kamolensis

Maui remya
Remya mauiensis

Alsinidendron trinerve

ko`oloa`ula
Abutilon menziesii

Cooke's koki`o
Kokia cookei

Viola lanaiensis

Cyanea macrostegia ssp. gibsonii

ma`oli`oli
Schiedea apokremnos

haha
Cyanea copelandii ssp. copelandii

Cyanea undulata

popolo `aiakeakua
Solanum sandwicense

Cyanea superba

pilo
Hedyotis mannii

Hawaiian vetch
Vicia menziesii

kio`ele
Hedyotis coriacea

Hedyotis degeneri

kauila
Colubrina oppositifolia

kaulu
Pteralyxia kauaiensis

Diellia falcata

nehe
Lipochaeta micrantha

Haplostachys haplostachya var. angustifolia

clay-loving wild-buckwheat
Eriogonum pelinophilum

nehe
Lipochaeta waimeaensis

pallid sturgeon
Scaphirhynchus albus

Osterhout milk-vetch
Astragalus osterhoutii

golden-cheeked warbler
Dendroica chrysoparia

Ash Meadows Amargosa pupfish
Cyprinodon nevadensis mionectes

crenulate lead-plant
Amorpha crenulata

Cumberland bean pearlymussel
Villosa trabalis

Kearney's blue-star
Amsonia kearneyana

Cumberland sandwort
Arenaria cumberlandensis

yellow-blossom pearlymussel
Epioblasma florentina florentina

Mexican long-nosed bat
Leptonycteris nivalis

Carolina northern flying squirrel
Glaucomys sabrinus coloratus

tubercled-blossom pearlymussel
Epioblasma torulosa torulosa

 Florida grasshopper sparrow
Ammodramus savannarum floridanus

Amargosa vole
Microtus californicus scirpensis

California freshwater shrimp
Syncaris pacifica

Big Bend gambusia
Gambusia gaigei

Etonia rosemary
Conradina etonia

Brooksville bellflower
Campanula robinsiae

Okeechobee gourd
Cucurbita okeechobeensis ssp. okeechobeensis

sandplain gerardia
Agalinis acuta

Morro Bay kangaroo rat
Dipodomys heermanni morroensis

scrub mint
Dicerandra frutescens

Yuma clapper rail
Rallus longirostris yumanensis

slender-petaled musta...
Thelypodium stenopetalum

 rice rat
Oryzomys palustris natator

palmate-bracted bird's-beak
Cordylanthus palmatus

White River springfish
Crenichthys baileyi baileyi

Delmarva Peninsula fox squirrel
Sciurus niger cinereus

Anthony's riversnail
Athearnia anthonyi

Hualapai Mexican vole
Microtus mexicanus hualpaiensis

white cat's paw pearlymussel
Epioblasma sulcata delicata

Maguire daisy
Erigeron maguirei var. maguirei

Alabama lamp mussel
Lampsilis virescens

sockeye salmon
Oncorhynchus nerka

Pacific pocket mouse
Perognathus longimembris pacificus

Curtis' pearlymussel
Epioblasma florentina curtisi

 Hawaiian crow
Corvus hawaiiensis

Ozark big eared bat
Plecotus townsendii ingens

upland combshell
Epioblasma metastriata

Fresno kangaroo rat
Dipodomys nitratoides exilis

turgid-blossom pearlymussel
Epioblasma turgidula

coyote ceanothus
Ceanothus ferrisae

Cushenbury buckwheat
Eriogonum ovalifolium var. vineum

Pismo clarkia
Clarkia speciosa immaculata

Tiburon jewelflower
Streptanthus niger

Presidio clarkia
Clarkia franciscana

Pennell's bird's-beak
Cordylanthus tenuis ssp. capillaris

Tiburon paintbrush
Castilleja affinis ssp. neglecta

Santa Clara Valley dudleya
Dudleya setchellii

Cushenbury milk-vetch
Astragalus albens

California seablite
Suaeda californica

San Bernardino Mountains bladderpod
Lesquerella kingii ssp. bernardina

San Mateo woolly sunflower
Eriophyllum latilobum

fountain thistle
Cirsium fontinale var. fontinale

laukahi kuahiwi
Plantago princeps

ma`o hau hele
Hibiscus brackenridgei

Spermolepis hawaiiensis

arroyo southwestern toad
Bufo microscaphus californicus

Mann's bluegrass
Poa mannii

Bonamia menziesii

 southwestern willow flycatcher
Empidonax traillii extimus

Conservancy fairy shrimp
Branchinecta conservatio

Appalachian elktoe
Alasmidonta raveneliana

longhorn fairy shrimp
Branchinecta longiantenna

Metcalf Canyon jewelflower
Streptanthus albidus ssp.

asplenium-leaved diellia
Diellia erecta

pendant kihi fern
Adenophorus periens

Neraudia sericea

pauoa
Ctenitis squamigera

Diplazium molokaiense

alani
Melicope adscendens

alani
Melicope ovalis

 Morro shoulderband snail
Helminthoglypta walkeriana

rock gnome lichen
Gymnoderma lineare

spruce-fir moss spider
Microhexura montivaga

Etowah darter
Etheostoma etowahae

Texas ayenia
Ayenia limitaris

south Texas ambrosia
Ambrosia cheiranthifolia

Hedyotis parvula

haha
Cyanea lobata

Diellia unisora

ha`iwale
Cyrtandra polyantha

Phyllostegia waimeae

Hilo ischaemum
Ischaemum byrone

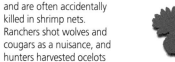

Nellie cory cactus
Escobaria minima

The common link shared by these species is that they are all hunted by man. Many of the plants, especially cacti like the Nellie cory and Knowlton, are prized by collectors. The sea turtles are sought for their meat and eggs throughout the Caribbean and are often accidentally killed in shrimp nets. Ranchers shot wolves and cougars as a nuisance, and hunters harvested ocelots for their pelts.

Bachman's warbler
Vermivora bachmanii

Wright fishhook cactus
Sclerocactus wrightiae

eastern cougar
Felis concolor couguar

Harper's beauty
Harperocallis flava

Kemp's ridley sea turtle
Lepidochelys kempii

red wolf
Canis rufus

Eskimo curlew
Numenius borealis

smooth coneflower
Echinacea laevigata

Davis' green pitaya
Echinocereus viridiflorus var. davisii

Mitchell's satyr butterfly
Neonympha mitchellii mitchellii

Arizona agave
Agave arizonica

star cactus
Astrophytum asterias

lanai sandalwood
Santalum freycinetianum var. lanaiense

Brady pincushion cactus
Pediocactus bradyi

Pima pineapple cactus
Coryphantha scheeri var. robustispina

San Rafael cactus
Pediocactus despainii

gray wolf
Canis lupus

hawksbill sea turtle
Eretmochelys imbricata

Sneed pincushion cactus
Coryphantha sneedii var. sneedii

Kuenzler hedgehog cactus
Echinocereus fendleri var. kuenzleri

ocelot
Felis pardalis

Minnesota trout lily
Erythronium propullans

green sea turtle
Chelonia mydas

Arizona hedgehog cactus
Echinocereus triglochidiatus var. arizonicus

Chapman rhododendron
Rhododendron chapmanii

Lloyd's hedgehog cactus
Echinocereus lloydii

leatherback sea turtle
Dermochelys coriacea

uhiuhi
Caesalpinia kavaiense

Uncompahgre fritillary butterfly
Boloria acrocnema

Nichol's Turk's head cactus
Echinocactus horizonthalonius var. nicholii

Knowlton cactus
Pediocactus knowltonii

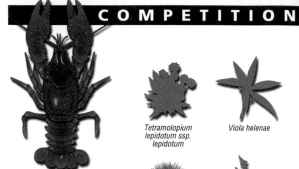

Shasta crayfish
Pacifastacus fortis

When an alien species is introduced to an ecosystem, the newcomer often crowds out the natives. California's Shasta crayfish, for example, has rapidly lost ground to non-native crayfish that reproduce much faster. And in Virginia the populous red-backed salamander is encroaching on areas held by the rarer Shenandoah salamander. But the biggest problem is in Hawaii, where plants that have evolved to fit narrow ecological niches are quickly overwhelmed by species from the mainland. Molasses grass—brought to Hawaii to create pastureland for deer and goats—has been particularly disruptive, as it grows rapidly and smothers the local flora in its wake.

Tetramolopium lepidotum ssp. lepidotum

Viola helenae

Ka`u silversword
Argyroxiphium kauense

Phyllostegia mollis

Stenogyne kanehoana

ha`iwale
Cyrtandra munroi

Gouania meyenii

large-flowered fiddleneck
Amsinckia grandiflora

Abutilon eremitopetalum

San Clemente Island broom
Lotus dendroideus ssp. traskiae

slender rush-pea
Hoffmannseggia tenella

Phyllostegia glabra var. lanaiensis

San Clemente loggerhead shrike
Lanius ludovicianus mearnsi

Hawaiian duck
Anas wyvilliana

Tetramolopium remyi

 Silene perlmanii

 Tobusch fishhook cactus *Ancistrocactus tobuschii*

Xylosma crenatum

 alani *Melicope mucronulata*

 Kauai hau kuahiwi *Hibiscadelphus distans*

 Abutilon sandwicense

Peter's Mountain mallow *Iliamna corei*

 MacFarlane's four-o'clock *Mirabilis macfarlanei*

 mahoe *Alectryon macrococcus*

 Lysimachia lydgatei

 `ihi`ihi *Marsilea villosa*

 `akoko *Chamaesyce celastroides var. kaenana*

shale barren rock-cress *Arabis serotina*

 Hesperomannia lydgatei

 Johnston's frankenia *Frankenia johnstonii*

Alsinidendron obovatum

 `akoko *Chamaesyce kuwaleana*

 nehe *Lipochaeta lobata var. leptophylla*

 `aiea *Nothocestrum peltatum*

Sacramento prickly-poppy *Argemone pleiacantha ssp. pinnatisecta*

 Aleutian shield-fern *Polystichum aleuticum*

 alani *Melicope reflexa*

Canby's dropwort *Oxypolis canbyi*

Malheur wire-lettuce *Stephanomeria malheurensis*

 kamakahala *Labordia lydgatei*

 rock cress *Arabis perstellata*

 pamakani *Tetramolopium capillare*

Pteris lidgatei

roseate tern *Sterna dougallii dougallii*

 Mohave tui chub *Gila bicolor mohavensis*

 **Lange's metalmark butterfly** *Apodemia mormo langei*

Shenandoah salamander *Plethodon shenandoah*

DISEASE

Hawaii `akepa *Loxops coccineus coccineus*

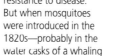 **large Kauai thrush** *Myadestes myadestinus*

Kauai `o`o *Moho braccatus*

small Kauai thrush *Myadestes palmeri*

Kauai `akialoa *Hemignathus procerus*

The five birds in this category are native to Hawaii, where they evolved with little resistance to disease. But when mosquitoes were introduced in the 1820s—probably in the water casks of a whaling ship—they began transferring avian pox and malaria from hardier alien birds to the native species. The Kauai Akialoa and Kauai `o`o may have already succumbed.

UNKNOWN

 **ashy dogweed** *Thymophylla tephroleuca*

Mariscus pennatiformis

popolo ku mai *Solanum incompletum*

shrubby reed-mustard *Schoenocrambe suffrutescens*

Scioto madtom *Noturus trautmani*

Although data are limited, slow reproduction and very low numbers appear to be the culprits for most of these species. In the two south Texas sites on which the ashy dogweed exists, botanists find few seedlings. And given the historically small population of the Scioto madtom—only 18 of the tiny catfish have ever been seen, and none since 1957—the species is probably already extinct.

FIVE BILLION TO ONE

By the time of her death at the Cincinnati Zoo in 1914, "Martha" was the world's last passenger pigeon. As many as five billion of the birds once ruled the skies over the Midwest, but relentless hunting reduced the population until it was too small to sustain itself.

What's at stake

Species at risk, and why

STATUS	Endangered
DATE LISTED	March 11, 1967
POPULATION	About 30-50 adults
HABITAT	Subtropical dense forests
CURRENT RANGE	South Florida
THREATS	Habitat destruction, inbreeding
PHOTOGRAPHED	Florida Panther National Wildlife Refuge (NWR), Naples, Fla.

Florida panther

This mangy Florida panther photographed itself by tripping an infrared beam. When wildlife biologists saw the photograph they were enthusiastic about over how much better the panther looked since they'd last seen it. Besides mange, "Number 51" is believed to be suffering from ringworm as well   diseases unknown in healthy populations of mountain lions elsewhere in the U.S. (Regionally, *Felis concolor coryi* is called mountain lion, cougar, puma, panther, painter, and just plain lion.)

More than a century of inbreeding has seriously depleted the panthers' gene pool, making them subject to disease, congenital defects, reproductive failure, and other calamities. Healthy cougars from west Texas have been introduced into the panther's south Florida range with the hope that interbreeding the subspecies will produce offspring with a healthier genetic mix. Ironically, saving this subspecies may well require diluting its genetic distinctiveness.

Because an adult panther needs a lot of room to roam, the available habitat in the Big Cypress Swamp and along the edges of the Everglades may never support many more than the 30 to 50 panthers now prowling south Florida's wildlands.

JOEL SARTORE WITH CATHERINE DEES (LEFT)

STATUS	Endangered
DATE LISTED	June 2, 1970
POPULATION	About 440
HABITAT	Great Plains prairie
CURRENT RANGE	Wyoming, Montana, South Dakota, Arizona
THREATS	Low numbers, habitat destruction, elimination of food supply (prairie dogs)
PHOTOGRAPHED	Sybille, Wyo. (left); U.L. Bend NWR, Mont. (below)

black-footed ferret

Having survived eons of predation by golden eagles, great horned owls, and coyotes, the black-footed ferret almost succumbed to the all-out war waged by humans on another species, the prairie dog. Ranchers and farmers spent decades destroying the prairie-dog towns of the Great Plains that fed and sheltered ferrets.

But it takes a lot of prairie dogs to sustain even a small population of ferrets, which eat little else. Its numbers frightfully reduced by the 1950s, the ferret was feared extinct in 1979, but a small population was discovered in Wyoming in 1981. Then a plague nearly wiped out the prairie dogs, followed closely by an epidemic of canine distemper in the ferret population. Down to 18 survivors in 1987, the ferret was brought in from the wild to a captive breeding program conducted by the Wyoming Department of Fish and Game, and rescued from certain extinction.

Ferrets bred in captivity at Sybille Canyon, Wyoming (left, where a sedated animal is being carried to its pen), are being returned to the wild in several states within the species' historic range, including Montana, South Dakota, and Arizona. The curious ferret at right takes a first look at its new, wild home in U.L. Bend National Wildlife Refuge, Montana.

STATUS	Threatened
DATE LISTED	October 9, 1975
POPULATION	Unknown
HABITAT	Vegetated streams with sandy bottoms
CURRENT RANGE	Tennessee River and tributaries
THREATS	Dam construction, water pollution
PHOTOGRAPHED	Cleveland, Tenn. (right); Lenoir City, Tenn. (below)

snail darter

The tranquil scene of a father and daughter fishing below the Tennessee River's Tellico Dam belies the controversy that once raged around the river, the dam, and an obscure, three-inch-long fish known as the snail darter. First discovered in a tributary of the Tennessee in 1973, and thought to occur nowhere else, the snail darter was listed as endangered in 1975. In the first test of the amended Endangered Species Act, the Supreme Court sided with the snail darter, halting construction of the Tellico Dam which threatened its habitat. The battle between conservationists and developers ended with Congress's exempting Tellico from the Endangered Species Act—consciously consigning a species to extinction.

The snail darter was transplanted to the nearby Hiwassee River, where the study specimen at right was photographed. Other populations were found in Tennessee, Georgia, and Alabama, and in 1984, the snail darter was reclassified from endangered to threatened.

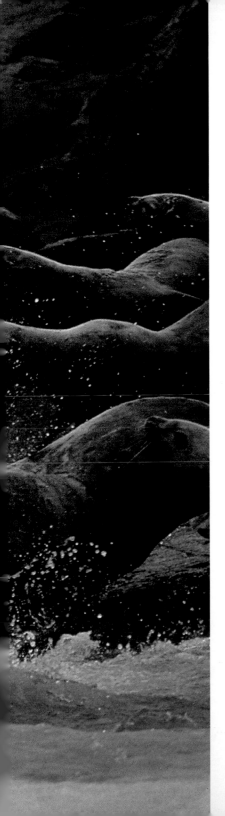

STATUS Threatened
DATE LISTED April 5, 1990
POPULATION About 116,000 (NOTE: This figure includes Soviet populations)
HABITAT North Pacific islands
CURRENT RANGE North Pacific Ocean and Arctic Ocean
THREATS Unclear; depletion of food sources is a likely factor
PHOTOGRAPHED Lowrie Island, Alas.

Steller sea lion

This largest of the eared seals is one imposing, fish-eating predator. But it's no match for seagoing trawlers, which have decimated North Pacific stocks of walleye pollock, the Steller sea lion's favorite food. That may explain its precipitous decline in recent years, after having survived centuries of hunting by native peoples and more than a hundred years of intensive commercial hunting (for meat, hides, blubber, and oil), as well as persecution by human fishermen whose catches they sometimes raided.

Even so, the Steller's very lionlike roar could be heard throughout its historic range around the North Pacific Rim from Hokkaido in northern Japan to Año Nuevo Island in central California. The species survives there still, but in the central part of its range—the Gulf of Alaska and the Aleutian Islands, where more than 75 percent of the population once lived—its numbers have plummeted over the past quarter century.

On Lowrie Island in the Alaska panhandle, where these subadult males were photographed, as many as 5,000 Steller sea lions congregate during the height of the summer breeding and pupping season. Farther south, the population is also stable or increasing. Why these animals are doing so much better than other seals to the north and west is something biologists very much want to find out.

STATUS	Threatened
DATE LISTED	September 28, 1989
POPULATION	At least 17,000
HABITAT	Tallgrass prairie
CURRENT RANGE	Midwest
THREATS	Habitat destruction and fragmentation
PHOTOGRAPHED	Valentine, Nebr.

western prairie fringed orchid

With almost all of its tallgrass prairie habitat disappearing—having been converted for use as cropland, pasture, or for commercial development—the western prairie fringed orchid was listed as threatened in 1989. Then, biologists monitoring the scattered, relict

stands—marked to warn farmers away—discovered that 55 to 89 percent of the remaining orchids failed to reappear each spring. The insect required to pollinate the fragrant orchid—the long-tongued hawkmoth whose tongue is long enough and whose eyes are widely enough separated to get and carry the pollen from the orchids' exceptionally long nectar spurs—is also in short supply, largely because the orchid's habitat is now too widely fragmented for the moths to travel from one stand of orchids to another. (The wood-boring beetle shown here simply coexists with the orchids, neither helping nor harming them.) Lately, the species has been disappearing because of the pesticides drifting from nearby croplands. And in some places an exotic weed called leafy spurge is now crowding orchids out of their little patches of near prairie.

STATUS	Endangered
DATE LISTED	March 11, 1967
POPULATION	About 109
HABITAT	Isolated rocky cliffs
CURRENT RANGE	Southern California
THREATS	Low numbers, loss of habitat, poisoning
PHOTOGRAPHED	Los Padres National Forest

California condor

Oblivious to the fundamental questions posed and the furor raised by their tenuous existence, these hungry, captive-bred juvenile condors eagerly feed on handouts from their human protectors in the California Condor Recovery Team. Every three days, biologists

chain part of a stillborn calf carcass to this rock in Los Padres National Forest—easy pickings free of the coyote poisons, lead bullets and shotgun pellets, pesticides, and other carrion contaminants that almost exterminated the condor.

The 1986 decision to capture all the remaining condors for a last-ditch captive-breeding program raised troubling questions about the role of natural extinction in evolution and wildlife conservation— questions with which the wildlife community was ill prepared to wrestle. Condors are now being returned to the wild and to a world in which they were already declining before Europeans set foot on this continent.

STATUS   Endangered in Florida; threatened elsewhere
DATE LISTED   July 28, 1978
POPULATION   Unknown
HABITAT   Pelagic; breeds on beaches
CURRENT RANGE   Pantropical in waters remaining above 68°F in the coldest month
THREATS   Destruction and alteration of nesting habitat (the beaches), disease, getting caught in fishing nets, hunting
PHOTOGRAPHED   South Padre Island, Tex.

green sea turtle

All sea turtles are threatened or endangered, but only the green
turtle is listed both ways: endangered in Florida and on the
Pacific coast of Mexico, threatened everywhere else. Sea turtles
have long been exploited for their edible eggs, succulent flesh,
and tannable skin, but the green turtle has also been prized for
"calipee" and "calipash," cartilaginous tissue attached to its shell
used to make green turtle soup. As if these deliberate
depredations weren't enough, great numbers of sea turtles are
drowned when they become entangled in shrimp trawls.
Shrimpers resist the use of turtle-excluding devices (TEDs),
sometimes violently. And remaining green turtles are now
threatened by a disease that may be caused by pollution.

    Green and other sea turtles prefer to nest on the same
warm, sandy beaches favored by sun-loving human beings and
real estate developers. Even when nesting sites aren't destroyed,
either by development or by trampling, hatchlings may be
disoriented by electric lights and wander in confusion while
predators have at them.

    Ila Loetscher, the "Turtle Lady" of South Padre Island,
Texas, is one of the professionals and volunteers licensed by the
federal government to handle and keep wildlife species, often
to rehabilitate them from injury.

STATUS Endangered
DATE LISTED June 1, 1976
POPULATION 5,000-10,000
HABITAT Coastal sand dunes
CURRENT RANGE Southern California
THREATS Urbanization
PHOTOGRAPHED El Segundo, Calif.

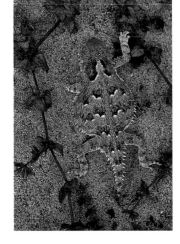

El Segundo blue butterfly

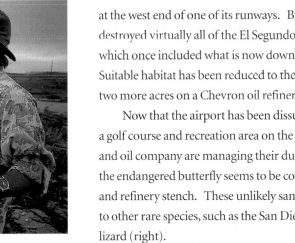

Noise pollution is a serious problem around many large airports. At Los Angeles International (LAX), it may have helped save an endangered butterfly from extinction. In the early 1970s, the LAX airport authority purchased and cleared about a thousand noise-afflicted houses from the area surrounding the sand dunes at the west end of one of its runways. By then, urban bloat had destroyed virtually all of the El Segundo blue butterfly's habitat, which once included what is now downtown Los Angeles. Suitable habitat has been reduced to the airport's 302 acres and two more acres on a Chevron oil refinery site just south of LAX.

Now that the airport has been dissuaded from building a golf course and recreation area on the dunes, and both airport and oil company are managing their dunes for conservation, the endangered butterfly seems to be coexisting with jet noise and refinery stench. These unlikely sanctuaries also are haven to other rare species, such as the San Diego coast horned lizard (right).

Still, troubles persist. Tumbleweeds, rye grass, and ice plant have invaded the dunes, threatening to choke out the wild buckwheat that is all the El Segundo's caterpillar eats. But LAX, Chevron, governments, academic scientists, and volunteers like this one about to plant critical vegetation (left) are working cooperatively to fight off these threats.

STATUS	Endangered
DATE LISTED	Various
POPULATION	Unknown
HABITAT	Fresh water rivers and streams
CURRENT RANGE	Illinois, Indiana, Ohio, Kentucky, Tennessee, West Virginia, Virginia
THREATS	Pollution, dam construction
PHOTOGRAPHED	Kyles Ford, Tenn.

fanshell mussel

Lacking the fuzzy appeal of small mammals, the charisma of large predators, the beauty of birds, or the recreational allure of fish, freshwater mussels register low when it comes to human awareness. Barely noticed in abundance, hardly missed in decline, these humble bivalves have become among the most endangered American species. These endangered fanshells, and the Cumberland combshell (a candidate for endangered listing) they flank, are from Kyles Ford on the Clinch River in Tennessee, which has more species of freshwater mussels than are found in all of Europe. At least for now.

Dams, siltation, agricultural runoff, acid mine drainage, industrial pollution, and heated discharges have all played roles in the declining fortunes of fresh water mussels. Additionally, the pearl button industry mined our mussel beds for more than half a century, until the development of better plastic buttons.

According to the American Fisheries Society, fewer than a fourth of the country's nearly 300 mussel species are stable; the rest are threatened (6 species), endangered (51), extinct (20), or declining (74).

STATUS	Endangered
DATE LISTED	March 11, 1967
POPULATION	250-285
HABITAT	Forests, swamps, and coastal prairies
CURRENT RANGE	North Carolina, Tennessee
THREATS	Reduction in habitat, hybridization
PHOTOGRAPHED	Graham, Wash. (left); Alligator River NWR, N.C. (below)

red wolf

The first endangered species for which a recovery plan was put in place, and the first predatory mammal ever reintroduced to the wild, the red wolf has rebounded from just 17 animals to approximately 300. From captive-breeding facilities such as this one at Point Defiance Zoo in Tacoma, Washington (where mother and pup were photographed), red wolves have been released on public wildlands in North Carolina and Tennessee, where they are now breeding. If they stray too far, they are "soft-trapped" (right) and returned to their isolation from human neighborhoods.

Having survived hunting, trapping, poisoning, the destruction or alteration of much of its original habitat, and the extinction of two of its three subspecies, the red wolf faces new peril. Recent DNA studies have failed to distinguish between red wolves and wolf-coyote hydrids. More studies, and a scientific review of endangered species management, are under way.

STATUS   Threatened
DATE LISTED   March 3, 1987
POPULATION   7,000-11,000
HABITAT   Scrub land
RANGE   Peninsular Florida
THREATS   Habitat destruction
PHOTOGRAPHED   Osprey, Fla.

Florida scrub jay

Third-generation real estate broker, self-taught naturalist, and indefatigable defender of Florida's disappearing scrub habitat, Jon Thaxton is almost single-handedly responsible for saving the 1,300-acre Mary Thaxton Memorial Preserve in Osprey, Florida, named for his mother. Major beneficiaries include some 100 Florida scrub jays in 25 family groups.

An isolated subspecies of the more common blue jay, the Florida bird depends entirely upon a type of habitat—sandy, flatland palmetto scrub with oak and pine trees stunted and thinned by periodic fires—that humans regard as worthless. So much of the state's scrub habitat has succumbed to clearing for real estate development on the coasts, and orange growing and cattle ranching inland, that the jays have been entirely eliminated from several counties. Some ornithologists had predicted the bird was heading for extinction. Now, thanks to determined defenders like Jon Thaxton, nascent state efforts, and federal protection of the species at Ocala National Forest and the space center and wildlife refuge at Cape Canaveral-Merritt Island, the Florida scrub jay's population is now considered relatively stable.

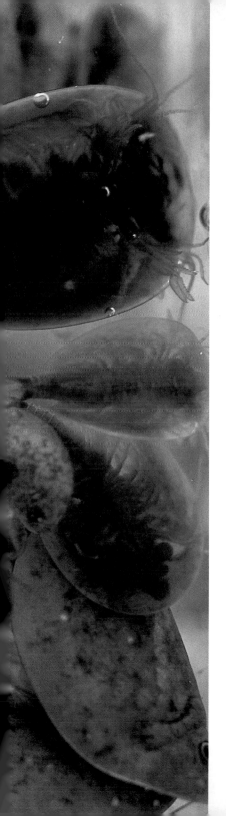

STATUS   Endangered
DATE LISTED   September 9, 1994
POPULATION   Unknown
HABITAT   Vernal pools and swales
CURRENT RANGE   Central Valley, California
THREATS   Habitat destruction, pollution
PHOTOGRAPHED   Kesterson NWR, near Los Banos, Calif.

vernal pool tadpole shrimp

Evolution has adapted these living fossils to drought, flood, heat, and cold, but vernal pool tadpole shrimp haven't been well prepared to cope with the ways of human beings. These bottom-scuttling creatures live just long enough to hatch, grow, mate, and lay eggs—maybe three months. Then the vernal pools in which they live dry up, and the unhatched eggs must wait several weeks, or even years in the dried muds of their ephemeral home pools.

A few eggs may be transplanted to other vernal pools on the legs of wading birds or in the mud-matted hair of mammals, which is why saving individual pools may not be enough, and why preservation of the pool complexes that define a population is so important to the species' survival. Other eggs succumb to water projects, urban sprawl, agriculture, roads, off-road vehicles—the forces that have destroyed some 90 percent of all the vernal pools in California's Central Valley, formerly prime habitat for the tadpole shrimp.

STATUS	Endangered
DATE LISTED	March 11, 1967
POPULATION	About 320
HABITAT	Wilderness wetlands
CURRENT RANGE	U.S. Rocky Mountains, U.S. and Canadian Great Plains, Florida
THREATS	Diminished habitat
PHOTOGRAPHED	Aransas NWR (left); Bosque del Apache NWR, N. Mex. (below)

whooping crane

Two decades of trying to establish a second wild flock of whooping cranes have resulted in bitter frustration. Hoping to augment the single small flock that breeds in Canada's Northwest Territory and winters on the Texas coast, wildlife biologists have been placing captive-bred whooper eggs in sandhill crane nests at Grays Lake National Wildlife Refuge in Idaho.

But predation, disease, and problems in migration, pair formation, and incubation have limited the second flock to just seven birds—including this genetically impure "whoophill" (right), a whooper-sandhill hybrid.

Although the whooping crane was one of the first species to be recognized as endangered, serious rescue attempts did not begin until the wild population had dipped to about 20 birds. One whooping crane biologist observed, "If you see a species on the slide, heading for the 'threatened' list, take remedial action now. It's a lot easier and a lot cheaper."

STATUS   Endangered
DATE LISTED   June 12, 1989
POPULATION   At least 850
HABITAT   Virgin woodlands, maritime scrub and grasslands
CURRENT RANGE   South Dakota, Nebraska, Oklahoma, Arkansas, Rhode Island, Massachusetts
THREATS   Low numbers, habitat alteration
PHOTOGRAPHED   Gothenburg, Nebr.

American burying beetle

Small enough to handle, yet large enough to supply the energy required, a mourning dove is just right for the American burying beetle prospecting it. Once spread through the mature forests of 32 states, the District of Columbia, and three Canadian provinces, the American burying beetle declined until it was known in only two sites in Oklahoma and Rhode Island. It has now been rediscovered in Arkansas, South Dakota, and Nebraska and reintroduced to an island in Massachusetts.

Having discovered carrion of suitable size, a mated pair will bury it several inches deep. (If the carcass is lying on ground that's too hard, the beetles will lie on their backs beneath the corpse and "walk" it upwards of ten feet to a better burial site.) After their eggs have been laid near the carrion, the male and female will remain to help care for the larvae—rare behavior among noncolonial insects.

Population size is unknown in most locations, but fewer than a thousand American burying beetles are thought to live in the Northeast—precious few for creatures that must happen upon dead animals of a certain size before skunks, opossums, raccoons, and other more numerous scavengers do.

STATUS	Endangered
DATE LISTED	June 2, 1970
POPULATION	At least 1,850
HABITAT	River mouths and inlets, coastal Atlantic Ocean and Gulf of Mexico
CURRENT RANGE	Florida, Georgia
THREATS	Powerboats, poaching, habitat loss
PHOTOGRAPHED	Crystal River, Fla.

Florida manatee

The West Indian manatee is one of the most endangered marine mammals in the coastal waters of the United States. The 1996 annual winter census of the Florida subspecies (*Trichechus manatus latirostris*) counted 2,274 manatees—400 more than had ever been

JOEL SARTORE WITH JOE STANCAMPIANO

recorded in Florida. Powerboat and development interests immediately opined that stronger conservation efforts were therefore unnecessary. A few weeks later, alarming numbers of otherwise healthy manatees were mysteriously dying, apparently from pneumonia, dramatically underscoring the fragile nature of the species' continuing survival.

Meanwhile, manatees continued as before to succumb to loss of habitat, collisions with speeding boats, and being crushed or drowned in floodgates and canal locks. Hooks, fishing lines, and other debris cause many injuries, and turbid runoff kills the sea grasses they eat. Harassment may also disturb mating and feeding, so Florida's Citrus County's policy of permitting divers to swim with and touch manatees generates great controversy.

STATUS	Endangered
DATE LISTED	January 17, 1984
POPULATION	About 200
HABITAT	Marshy areas
CURRENT RANGE	Laramie basin, Wyoming
THREATS	Herbicides, pesticides, predation, irrigation practices
PHOTOGRAPHED	Sybille, Wyo.

Wyoming toad

The Wyoming toad was discovered in fairly abundant quantities in 1946, its range limited to the Laramie Basin of Wyoming. Following a drastic population decline in the early 1970s, the toad was feared extinct in 1984. The species was rediscovered in 1987, and captive breeding was started soon thereafter. Captive-bred adults released into a new location in the wild in 1992 succumbed to red leg disease, which destroys the immune system, decimating the toads. In 1994, 14 toads in captivity produced 6,000-8,000 eggs but only 20-30 tadpoles. Today, there are no known Wyoming toads in the wild, and the captive population numbers about 200.

The reasons for this disappointing history are not entirely clear. Amphibian captive breeding programs are one of wildlife management's most challenging problems. In the wild, herbicide and pesticide spraying in toad habitat to control weeds and mosquitoes, the increase in predators, water pollution, and changes in weather patterns are all factors in the toad's declining fortunes.

STATUS Formerly endangered; now delisted
DATE LISTED Listed as endangered June 2, 1970; delisted June 15, 1994
POPULATION About 23,100
HABITAT Pelagic
CURRENT RANGE Pacific Ocean and Arctic Ocean
THREATS Human predation
PHOTOGRAPHED Laguna San Ignacio, Baja, Mexico

gray whale

The gray whale's recovery and delisting isn't the Endangered Species Act's only success story, but it's one of the relatively few so far. When the whale was listed as endangered in 1970, its population was estimated at 12,567. At its delisting in 1994, the population estimate was 23,109—at least as many as existed prior to commercial whaling in the 19th century. Ongoing protection for the species continues to be assured through the Marine Mammal Protection Act. The recovery of the eastern Pacific population of the gray whale must be considered in the sobering context of all four populations or subspecies: Some scientists fear the western Pacific population is now extinct, joining the two Atlantic subspecies which disappeared in the 1700s.

Of the 984 U.S. species that have been listed as endangered or threatened since the act was passed in 1973,

- 9 species have been removed for technical reasons.
- 7 species have been reclassified from threatened to endangered, and 20 from endangered to threatened.
- 7 species have been declared extinct.
- 8 species have recovered and are no longer endangered: Rydberg milk-vetch, Palau dove, Palau owl, Palau fantail flycatcher, brown pelican, Arctic peregrine falcon, American alligator, and gray whale.

HUMBOLDT COUNTY, CALIFORNIA, 1909

The advent of the timber industry spelled disaster for hundreds of species that make their homes in the forest. Logging in the Pacific Northwest has devastated species ranging from the spotted owl, which lives in the trees, to salmon, which must contend with muddy runoff from clear-cut areas.

It's the habitat

Three ecosystems under seige

The Pacific Northwest

ABUNDANT RAIN AND FOG HAVE BLESSED the Pacific Northwest with luxuriant forests of ancient trees, teeming with woodland creatures, and with rushing rivers full of cold, clear water and silvery salmon. But all that is fast becoming past tense. Salmon are now in imminent peril and environmental pessimists doubt they'll ever return to their former abundance, if they survive at all. Droughts in recent years have sharpened the competition for water among salmon fisheries, electric utilities, and irrigated agriculture. The region's ancient forests and the creatures they shelter aren't in much better shape. Log exports to Japan, while lucrative (without providing sawmill jobs), increase timber demands on the region's national forests. Many of the Pacific Northwest's environmental troubles are laid at the feet of timber and timber products, the region's dominant industries, but public power, agriculture, and mining also contribute to the challenges facing the region's habitat.

Media attention in recent years has been focused on salmon and the northern spotted owl, but the region has plenty of other imperiled species. Oregon, perhaps not coincidentally the state most heavily dependent on timber, has 28 listed species; Washington, 18; Idaho, 15. California has 162 species on the list, but most are from the southern half of the state. The region's listed creatures include brown (grizzly) bear, woodland caribou, marbled murrelet, western snowy plover, bald eagle, American peregrine falcon, Aleutian Canada goose, leatherback, olive ridley and green sea turtles, Oregon silverspot butterfly (found in all four states), several chubs and suckers, white sturgeon and six snail species in Idaho, three subspecies of trout in California (one of which, the Lahontan cutthroat, is also listed in Oregon), and the California red-legged frog, perhaps the protagonist of Mark Twain's "The Celebrated Jumping Frog of Calaveras County." Most of the listed plants are from restricted habitats, but water howellia (a bellflower) is listed in all states.

While habitats remain unprotected, species continue to decline.

INDIAN
HEAVEN
WILDERN...

SPOTTED OWL
No other endangered species has so bitterly polarized conservation and commercial interests. Not the simplistic "owls vs. jobs" caricature presented in the media, the issue raises complex questions of forest ecology and economics.

CLEAR-CUTTING
Like so many patches of mange on the flanks of Mt. Adams, these clear-cuts in Gifford Pinchot National Forest stand in speckled contrast to the verdant wholeness of the Indian Heaven Wilderness.

SALMON
Their rivers controlled for the benefit of power generation and agricultural irrigation, and their tributary spawning beds silted by erosion, damaged by road-building, and warmed by sunlight no longer filtered by the forest canopy—all thanks to clear-cut logging—the Columbia Basin's salmon are barely hanging on.

DAMS
Fish ladders on dams such as Bonneville and The Dalles enable salmon to make their upstream spawning runs. But the dams and their reservoirs keep many juvenile salmon from ever reaching the sea. Chinook salmon from the Snake River, the Columbia's largest tributary, are already listed as threatened, and its sockeye salmon, as endangered.

LANDSAT TERRAIN MODEL PROCESSED BY PACIFIC MERIDIAN RESOURCES
IN COOPERATION WITH THE USDA FOREST SERVICE, REGION 6

LOOKING LIKE THE LIFELESS MOONSCAPES and war-ravaged battlefields to which they are often likened, clear-cuts—like this 240-acre cut—on erodible slopes in Washington State's Olympic Peninsula blight the forest in many ways. They remove ancient trees that provide the habitat needed by cavity-nesting birds and other species. They disrupt the complex fabric of life found only in undisturbed old-growth forests. They remove the shady canopy that keeps temperatures suitable for creatures in the understory and on the forest floor and especially for spawning salmon and trout in the creeks and tributaries. They intensify the soil erosion, already begun by the construction of logging roads, that chokes the streams and covers the spawning beds with silt. And they fragment the forest ecosystem, disrupting its processes and degrading the habitat value of uncut patches between them.

"THE BILLION-DOLLAR BIRD" is how loggers sometimes disparage the northern spotted owl. Preservation and recovery plans for the owl, which depends on undisturbed old-growth forest, threaten to discomfit or disrupt a traditional industry that is already in decline because of mill automation, bottom-line cost-cutting, over harvesting on private timberlands in the region, and other factors unrelated to endangered-species protection.

WITH NATURAL FISH POPULATIONS PLUMMETING, huge sums are spent each year to raise salmon and steelhead (anadromous rainbow trout) in hatcheries. Juvenile fish so expensively produced suffer great mortality. This steelhead being pumped from an Idaho hatchery will be trucked to a stream before being released to make its way through reservoirs and dams on its way to the sea. The dams have turned the Columbia River into a chain of sluggish lakes, where squawfish and other predators thrive, gorging themselves on the young salmon. When the floodgates are opened to draw down the reservoirs in high-water years (as shown here at Bonneville Dam in mid-March 1996), passage is relatively simple.

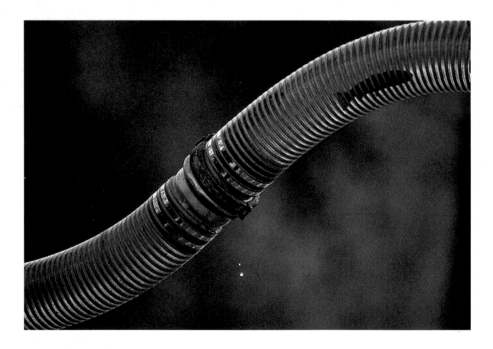

THIS NATIVE AMERICAN DIP-NETTER went fishless at his
traditional salmon-fishing spot on the Klickitat River, a tributary
which enters the Columbia between the Dalles and Bonneville
dams. Sport anglers and commercial fishermen suffer similar results.
In 1995 the Bonneville Fish Hatchery produced 30 million chinook
salmon smolts like these. But government cutbacks are closing
hatcheries and forcing those remaining to limit their production.

URBAN SPRAWL
In its sprawl, Los Angeles is virtually indistinguishable from its county, which includes more than 80 other cities—as well as 900 square miles of desert habitat—within its 4,083 square miles.

CALIFORNIA GNATCATCHER
With some of the world's most valuable real estate—up to $3 million an acre—for habitat, the threatened coastal California gnatcatcher's protection has become a particularly volatile issue.

DESERT DEVELOPMENT
Decades of putting people where only desert-adapted species can eke out a living and wresting water from distant sources to sprinkle lawns and fill swimming pools have exacted a heavy toll on desert habitats and species.

DESERT TORTOISE
Grazing livestock, off-road joyriders, and urban developers continue to destroy the desert tortoise's arid habitat.

SAN BERNARDINO MTS.

SAN GABRIEL MTS.

LOS ANGELES

N

PACIFIC OCEAN

LANDSAT TERRAIN MODEL PROCESSED BY RISE GEOTECHNICS, SANTA BARBARA, CALIFORNIA

The Desert Southwest

THE AMERICAN SOUTHWEST IS NOT one vast, unbroken expanse of desert. It is a complex of many arid and semiarid environments. "A semidesert with a desert heart," the Texas historian Walter Prescott Webb called it. The desert Southwest contains three major deserts and life zones—Great Basin, Mojave, and Sonoran—separated by and interspersed with a myriad of habitats and microenvironments. The limited water that defines desert or semidesert also shapes its suitability as habitat.

With the warming that followed the retreat of the Pleistocene glaciers, some plants and animals retreated to milder patches of habitats in the mountains and valleys, where evolutionary isolation separated them still further from their relatives elsewhere. Others evolved to thrive in the great heat and dryness of deserts where nothing else could live. Still others wax and wane with seasonal or longer-term fluctuations in drought and moisture.

Man moved into this inhospitable environment, convinced that water could always be found somewhere and moved to where it was needed. Virtually everywhere that people went, rivers were dewatered, groundwater tables were lowered, and riparian habitats were destroyed by dessication or trampling livestock. With water and liveable habitat in the desert so scarce, and sight lines in these open spaces so long, the results of resource competition and environmental degradation are more readily apparent than they are elsewhere. No longer able to ignore the problems, we have finally begun to plan for peaceful coexistence with the Southwest's native species.

LOS ANGELES and its satellites (such as this subdivision in Orange County) have continued to grow, following the path of least physiographic resistance and biggest return on the dollar, choking the Los Angeles Basin with houses, swimming pools, shopping centers, freeways, and parking lots. The region's wildlife has retreated into what is left: hardscrabble canyons, unstable slopes, hillsides covered with shrubby tinder. Supply and demand being what it is, developers have now turned to those once unpromising sites, the last habitat for some of the state's 162 species listed as threatened or endangered.

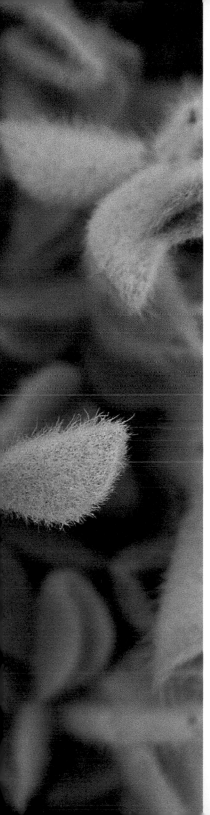

RESCUED from development by the Nature Conservancy and the U.S. Fish and Wildlife Service, the Ash Meadows milkvetch (threatened) and the Ash Meadows speckled dace (endangered) may live on. They are among the 24 species unique to a wetland oasis within the sagebrush desert of the Mojave west of Las Vegas. Leg-banded by biologists studying the impact of development in their oasis of habitat within the asphalt desert of Los Angeles Basin, this mist-netted coastal California gnatcatcher fared less well. Two days after being displaced by bulldozers, none of the banded birds could be found and were presumed dead.

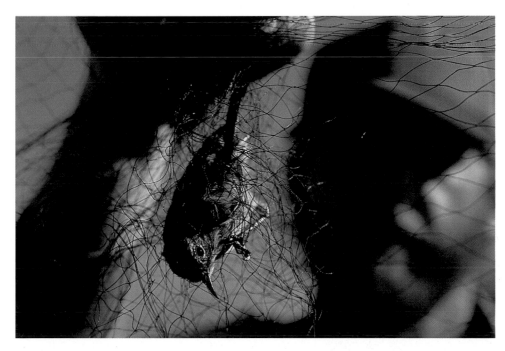

A "REFUGEE" is held aloft at the tiny Desert Tortoise Conservation Center near Las Vegas. Environmental consultants—this one is monitoring a bulldozer "enhancing" the California desert for a gambling casino being built by the Fort Mojave Indian Tribe—rescue tortoises being displaced by development and send them to the Tortoise Conservation Center where they are put up for "adoption" by human foster families, turned over to scientific research, or euthanized. They can't be relocated to suitable habitat protected in a handful of preserves because male tortoises are extremely territorial.

93

Florida

WATER, WETLANDS, WOODS, AND WILDLIFE virtually define Florida. Its tidal shoreline—
8,426 miles of it—is second in total length only to Alaska's, and its boundaries enclose some
4 million acres of water. But 2.8 million acres are inland waters, including some 1,700 streams,
30,000 lakes, and one of the world's great wetlands, the Everglades. Roughly half
the state is in forest—including southern swamp forests and upland scrub, both
rich in wildlife. Florida's wildlife bounty includes nearly 100 species of mammals,
more than 400 species and subspecies of birds, hundreds of species of fish and
shellfish, and countless species of plants, insects, and other invertebrates.

Florida also has roughly 14 million people, about 250 people per square mile, most of
them crowded into the state's coastal lowlands. As it has for decades, the state's
population is growing apace, up more than 40 percent since 1980. And that's why
97 of Florida's species are listed as threatened or endangered.

When people settle in or around wetlands, they start draining,
ditching, dredging, and filling them, moving the water all around.
They turn the wetlands into crop and grazing lands,
residential and commercial real estate. They destroy it as
wildlife habitat if not altogether. Nationally, wetlands are
habitat for some 600 species of animals and 5,000 plant species. Nearly half
of all the animal species listed as threatened or endangered in the U.S., and more than a
quarter of our listed plant species, are dependent upon wetlands for at least part of each year. Over
the last 200 years, Florida has lost nearly half its wetlands, more than 9 million acres all told, more
wetland acres than have been lost by any other state.

Wildlife conservation in America began in Florida at the start of this century, when citizens
banded together to save the snowy egret from plume hunters and the millinery trade, and when
President Theodore Roosevelt established the first national wildlife refuge at Pelican Island. As the
century ends, the ultimate fate of Florida's, and America's, wildlife still hangs in the balance.

AGRICULTURE
Swampland farming requires the disruption of natural patterns of water movement and pooling, and the application of fertilizers and pesticides that affect water quality.

FLORIDA PANTHER
Once found from Texas to Tennessee and South Carolina, the Florida panther's habitat has been reduced by highways and other human encroachments and is now restricted to portions of the Big Cypress Swamp (east of area shown) and the edge of the Everglades.

WADING BIRDS
Loss of freshwater and brackish wetland habitat and artificial management of remaining wetlands in Florida have made the wood stork Florida's most endangered wading bird. Preservation of other wetlands, such as this one at Rookery Bay, suggest a rosier future for herons and egrets.

HOUSING
With more than three million new people to house each decade, Florida has dredged, ditched, drained, and pumped its way into trouble. The surface water flows needed to sustain its luscious habitats have been disrupted and its freshwater aquifer is increasingly infiltrated by salty sea water.

MARCO

GULF OF MEXICO

SPOT IMAGE PROCESSED BY THOMAS LO, SOUTH FLORIDA WATER MANAGEMENT DISTRICT

BY DAWN'S EARLY LIGHT, DC-3s from Lee County's mosquito-control air force (which includes 11 helicopters) lay down a lethal rain of Malathion, Resmethrin, and diesel fuel over Fort Myers, one of the consequences of putting large numbers of people in swamp country. Besides mosquitoes, which are near the bottom of the Everglades and Big Cypress food webs, the pesticides also kill large numbers of butterflies and other insects which are either beneficial or upon which Florida's wildlife ultimately depends. Wetland drainage, even more damaging than spraying, has also been widely practiced in Florida in the name of mosquito control.

FLORIDA POPULATION trends: A human population boom has sent wildlife populations plummeting. Human expansion nearly always entails displacement of wildlife from habitat. But management of Florida's wetlands for water supply, flood and mosquito control, irrigation, cultivation, and other human purposes has adversely affected wildlife habitat far removed from human habitation. Nesting habitat has been protected in Everglades National Park and the Audubon sanctuary at Corkscrew Swamp, yet wood storks have suffered a string of nesting failures. Unnatural alteration of water levels has depleted their food supplies during the nesting season.

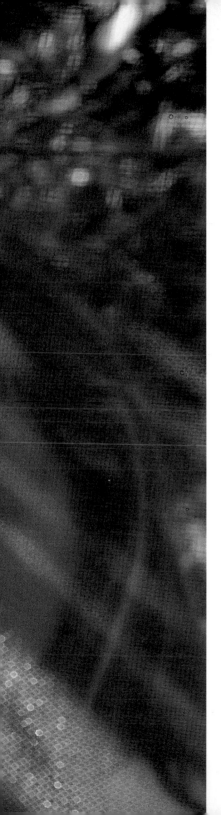

FLORIDA'S SCRUBLANDS are disappearing faster than its wetlands, having shrunk by nearly 90 percent over the last century. In the U.S. only 13 specimens of semaphore cactus are known to exist in the wild, yet the species isn't legally protected—even though 8 of them must be enclosed in mesh so they won't be killed by an exotic moth (opposite). Some 10,000 acres of scrubland remain in central Florida's Lake Wales Ridge, where a national wildlife refuge was created in 1994 to protect the large number of threatened and endangered species found here and nowhere else. Shown here (top to bottom), cutthroat grass, Edison's St. John's-wort, and the perforate reindeer moss (a lichen).

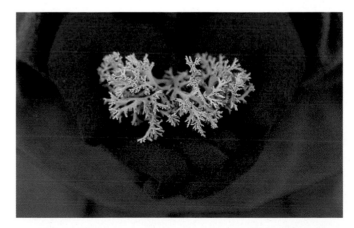

PUSHED INTO tiny corners of habitat, some species are prime candidates for calamity. In the U.S. the reclusive American crocodile (even more endangered in its Caribbean and Latin American range) now nests only on the margins of Florida Bay in Everglades National Park. Hide hunters had decimated it throughout its range. The endangered Florida Key deer, protected in a refuge named for it on Big Pine and surrounding keys, hasn't been hunted since 1939, but human beings still continue to kill it—with their cars. Its habitat shot through with roads and housing development, the Key deer succumbs to cars each year at a rate that's about equal to the birth rate.

BUFFALO'S GRAVEYARD

A mountain of buffalo skulls awaits processing into fertilizer on a Detroit farm on the bank of the Rouge River around 1895. At least 30 million of the shaggy creatures once thundered across the Great Plains, but hunters slaughtered them so relentlessly that by the 1890s only about a thousand were left. Now, thanks to careful conservation, about 200,000 buffalo roam in national parks like Yellowstone and in private herds.

The company we keep

Understanding the mess we're in

The Bold and the Beautiful

CONGRESS DID NOT BELIEVE THE TASK AHEAD would be easy when it unanimously passed the Endangered Species Act of 1973. But it seems unlikely that many of the legislators or their constituents understood just how complex the challenge of saving vanishing wildlife in the modern era would prove to be. For the most part, people imagined that the solutions lay in outlawing the hunting and trapping of hard-pressed species and perhaps creating a sanctuary or two to insulate them from human disturbances. That we might be called upon to share space and resources in a great many places, and that we might have to fundamentally reconsider the way we live on the land, would only become apparent as the years rolled on.

The rallying cries could be heard across the nation: Save the Sea Otters! Save the Whales! Save the Gators! Save the Grizzlies! Save the Wolves! Rescuing species was clearly the will of the people. Looking back, it is also clear that the early focus was on the kind of species ecologists refer to as charismatic megafauna—big critters with star appeal.

SAVE THE SEA OTTERS? Only the most hardened of hearts could resist this call. Beguiling and bewhiskered, the southern sea otter, *Enhydra lutris nereis,* is a fellow tool-user; floating on its back, a favorite position, the animal places shellfish on its chest and smashes them open with a rock held in its paw. Sleepy sea otters often wrap a strand of kelp around themselves so the current won't carry them away while they snooze. Unfortunately for the species, it wore the most valuable pelt among marine mammals. Fur hunters mined out herds once abundant from Washington to lower California. Official protection didn't come until 1910, and the last animal was believed killed in 1911, until a small group was discovered in 1938 in Monterey Bay.

This little band gradually expanded. The 1972 Marine Mammal Protection Act, followed by the ESA, shepherded the otters safely past angry abalone harvesters, who didn't like the competition from these natural divers. Sea otters eat far more clams, mussels, crabs, and sea urchins, and people soon noticed that the offshore kelp beds, which had been shrinking, were beginning to flourish again. The otters were gobbling the urchins that had been seriously overgrazing the kelp in the otters' absence. Because kelp forests are vital nursery areas for a great variety of marine organisms, including fish, there were all kinds of happy fishermen and amateur naturalists for every disgruntled abalone diver, even if many people didn't realize exactly why the sea life along the coast now seemed so much richer in places.

Sea otters lack a fat layer beneath their skin, relying instead on their plush fur and the air trapped within it for insulation. If oil pollution mats down this pelage, the animals lose their protection against the cold, as the spectacle of thousands of northern sea otters dying in the wake of the Exxon *Valdez* spill demonstrated all too clearly. The endangered status of southern sea otters was frequently raised in debates over offshore drilling along the California coast. In the end, the drilling proposals were defeated. To the degree that sea otter conservation played a role, the species may have once again helped ensure a better future for the fertile kelp beds and coastal life in general. By the early 1980s, the southern sea otter population had increased to around 1,300. They currently number more than 2,000, a success story by any measure.

SAVE THE WHALES? Can do. Not all whales, maybe, but at least gray whales. Well, not the Atlantic grays, which succumbed to the whaling fleets of the last century, but California gray whales. These marine mammals weigh up to 40 tons yet subsist chiefly on amphipods scarcely bigger than a fingernail paring. The mysterious pockmarks that divers noticed in many sea-bottom areas along the Pacific coast turn out to be places where gray whales have dug into the soft sediments with their heads to stir up meals of these shrimplike crustaceans.

Gray whales that summer in Arctic waters off Alaska and winter in lagoons along Mexico's Baja Peninsula complete one of the longest annual migrations of any mammal, a round trip of up to 12,000 miles. They return to the same shallow lagoons year after year to breed and rear their calves, probably because the shallow inlets offer an extra margin of safety from predators. But when whalers finally discovered these nursery areas during the mid-19th century, they became killing pools, their waters turning as red as the Baja sunsets.

The whalers called the gray whales devilfish, for they were the quarry most likely to ram boats and thrash them apart. What that name doesn't reveal is that the boat breakers were often trying to protect their young, which the men lanced first in order to draw mother whales closer.

From a low of a few thousand in the 1920s, the California gray whale population has increased to about 24,000, sufficiently recovered to

BADLANDS BIGHORN
Ovis canadensis auduboni

————

Last seen 1910

Once abundant throughout the Upper Great Plains, this close relative of the Rocky Mountain bighorn was hunted to extinction by the early 20th century.

————

have departed the endangered species list in June of 1994. In place of whaling, a much larger industry has grown up around simply enjoying the coast-hugging giants. Some 300,000 people spend five million dollars a year whale-watching in California alone. The activity is so popular that tour operators are being asked to develop guidelines so that the whales don't find themselves once again being hounded across the waters by boats full of people, even though they are waving cameras instead of harpoons.

Part of Baja's Laguna San Ignacio, a popular whale-watching spot, is entirely off-limits to visitors. Only a handful of commercial tour boats are permitted to travel the rest of the lagoon. Most of the whales tolerate human company, but there are always a few that seem to seek it out, like the mother whale that positioned her baby on her belly and then lifted it above the surface next to a boat, as if to show her young one to the visitors. Whatever the mother may have intended, she left a group of open-mouthed people with memories that would last all their lives.

While credit must also go to the International Whaling Commission, which banned the hunting of gray whales in 1937, and to Mexico, which established sanctuaries for the giants during that same decade, this is just the kind of outcome the ESA was designed to produce. The whales win and people win, and both will for generations to come.

SAVE THE GATORS? No problem. Like many reptiles, alligators lay large batches of eggs and have the potential to increase rapidly if protected. The Fish and Wildlife Service no sooner ran off poachers with aggressive law enforcement, levying fines of up to $25,000 as prescribed by the ESA, than *Alligator mississippiensis* began to bounce back.

In short order, gators were becoming a nuisance on golf courses and lawns in swamp-edge suburbs. By the 1980s a controlled commerce in meat and hides was allowed, and the species was downgraded from endangered to threatened. It would have been delisted altogether, but the Fish and Wildlife Service wanted to retain enough control over trade to protect the similar-looking, little-known, and highly endangered American crocodile along with imperiled crocodilians from other countries.

Our native U.S. crocodile, *Crocodylus acutus,* once reached lengths of 20 feet and beyond. Its snout is more slender than the American alligator's, and it favors more brackish water such as estuaries, feeding on fish, crabs, and waterbirds. When listed in 1975, the species had been reduced to perhaps 400, confined mainly to Florida's Cape Sable.

Because the crocodiles are a coastal species, they experienced habitat loss from shoreline construction in addition to heavy poaching. The diversion of water for irrigation, which threatens the Everglades, also reduces the amount of fresh water flowing into estuaries and tidal marshes, causing the areas to become too salty or, in some cases, too parched for the crocodiles and their food supply. This has slowed their comeback, for restoring the water that flows as a vast sheet down the southern half of the state is a far more complicated undertaking than policing poachers. Recently, however, both the numbers and range of the American crocodile appear to be expanding. A big female croc showed up not long ago in Ding Darling National Wildlife Refuge on Sanibel Island, many miles north of Cape Sable, and was reported thrashing the local gators as she laid claim to her new territory.

SAVE THE GRIZZLIES? Of course. These bears are a living definition of the word indomitable, the ultimate symbol of untamed wilderness. But adult males roam home ranges as large as a thousand square miles. In working to save grizzlies, we discovered that preserving enough space for them to survive raises its own set of obstacles to recovery.

Grizzlies are not necessarily creatures of rugged, mountain terrain to begin with. They could just as soon spend their time in lush valleys and river plains. Two centuries ago, they even flourished across much of the Great Plains and the Southwest. Nor were these bears really driven back into the mountains, as many folks seem to believe. They were just killed off everywhere else. Reduced from between 50,000 and 100,000 to fewer than 1,000 in the lower 48 states, *Ursus arctos horribilis* was declared threatened in 1975.

The wilderness we set aside for grizzlies consists largely of rocks, ice, and snow—the scenic high country that nobody had much commercial use for at the time. It offers inspiration to visitors but little for a several-hundred-pound omnivore to eat except during the brief mountain summer. Through spring and autumn, a grizzly trying to put on enough fat for winter hibernation is likely to be down at lower elevations, rambling with its humpbacked, slightly pigeon-toed, head-swinging gait onto what people consider their own home ranges.

The nation's best-known example of grizzly country, 2.5-million-acre Yellowstone National Park, is not really very good bear habitat. Most of it is a 6,000-foot-high plateau cloaked in relatively unproductive lodgepole pine forest and muffled beneath a deep snowpack from October into May. The surrounding countryside offers a richer, more diverse food supply. That is where many bears headed after the park closed its garbage dumps in the late 1960s, and where they met their death at the hands of people.

Today, the grizzly population within the six-million-acre Yellowstone ecosystem seems stable. Although some wildlife conservationists believe that optimistic figures provided by the government reflect an improvement in counting techniques rather than a true increase in population, the Fish and Wildlife Service estimates that there are more than 300 bears, of which some 65 are breeding-age females. Also encouraging are the results of blood and tissue analyses that indicate no loss of genetic diversity, always a concern in small, isolated populations.

An occasional silvertipped bear wanders down from Canada to take up residence in Washington's North Cascade Range. The Selkirk Range where Washington and Idaho meet near the Canadian border contains about three dozen bears. A little farther east, two or three dozen grizzlies linger in the Cabinet Mountains/Yaak Valley region of northwestern Montana, an area of intensive logging. For some time, the only breeding-age female known in the Cabinets was more than 30 years old. Biologists wanted to transplant eight females from British Columbia to shore up the population, but objections from nearby timber-based communities forced the Fish and Wildlife Service to reduce the number to four. They were brought in between 1991 and 1994. One died, and no sign of the others can be found.

The last place in the contiguous states that qualifies as grizzly country is also the best. Known among biologists as the Northern Continental Divide Ecosystem, or NCDE, it includes Glacier National Park, the Great Bear/Bob Marshall/Scapegoat Wilderness complex to the south, and adjoining Montana wildlands. Supporting an estimated 400 to 600 bears, it is linked to Canadian bear populations along the backbone of the Rockies.

Efforts to recover the species in these various ranges have increased regulations on grazing, logging, mining, oil and gas operations, road use, and even camping on millions of public acres such as national forests—and have created a fair amount of resentment. "One timber operation on a hillside doesn't hurt the bear that much," says the logger, "and people need the wood." "Show me the study proving that one new gas field is going to drive grizzlies to extinction," grouses the driller. "They have millions of other acres to roam." "How," asks the hiker, "can one more tent site do the grizzly in? Heck, I love bears." "What I'm doing won't make all that much difference either," says the subdivider turning

BLUE PIKE
Stizostedion vitreum glaucum

————

Last seen 1971

Fishermen pulled over a billion pounds of this species from Lake Erie between 1885 and 1962, precipitating a population crash from which it never recovered.

————

a sprawling ranch into a quiltwork of ranchettes. "It's just one place, and people want homes in the country." "There's nothing like living close to nature," exclaims the proud owner of a new cabin in the woods, "but can you please tell the wildlife department to come—soon!—and trap this bear that's been hanging around ever since it got into the dog food I left out on the porch."

"For bears," noted Chris Servheen, the Fish and Wildlife Service grizzly bear recovery coordinator, "private lands are the equivalent of mine fields." Although private property makes up less than five percent of current grizzly habitat, it is where more than three-quarters of all grizzlies are killed. Grizzlies also tend to start vanishing wherever there is more than a mile of road per square mile of land. Some move away to escape the increased disturbance; those that stay behind are more likely to have a fatal run-in with people. Though the road density in grizzly habitat within some national forests has declined since the bear was listed, pressure on undisturbed wildland acreage continues to increase.

Trying to keep further development at bay, conservationists have brandished the bear's threatened status time and again. The ESA makes an effective weapon, because it is less easily bent than other rules regarding natural resources on federal lands. But wherever the act succeeded in curtailing human activities, it made grizzlies the focus of even more resentment. Many Westerners who started off with a grudging admiration for the bears came to see them as emblems of environmental extremism and government interference with private enterprise.

Save the grizzly? Montana rancher Dick Christy thinks his constitutional rights got mauled somewhere along the way. In June 1982, after leasing land from the Blackfeet, he put 800 ewes and lambs out to graze on Chief Mountain, just east of Glacier Park. Christy encountered five grizzlies over the next month. Two, he learned, had been in trouble with livestock elsewhere and had been relocated on the mountain. All of them were eating his lamb chops.

Before the ESA the result would have been five dead bears. Times change. Eighty-four dead sheep after he started, Christy pulled out and sold off the rest of his flock. He figured his losses at more than $10,000. On top of that he was hit with a $2,500 fine, because he'd killed a grizzly. "We'd just bedded down the sheep and were having a cup of coffee when two bears came trotting toward the herd," he remembers. "I shot the lead one. I did it to protect my animals. But I could argue that I also fired in defense of my life, my wife's, and the herder's."

Christy spent another $60,000 on an unsuccessful legal appeal of his case. "I lost my rights as a private property owner," he insists. "Yet those bears were fully protected. I'm a victim of the Endangered Species Act."

For better or worse, these big, far-ranging carnivores now inhabit not only the Rockies and countless tall tales told around campfires but also the strange and surly realm of biopolitics. At public hearings on grizzly bear recovery, citizens shouted, "You're putting the needs of animals over those of people." Grizzlies as a whole aren't threatened, some pointed out. Only the population of the lower 48 states is shaky. Why should we have to modify our lifestyles in order to save them when Canada and Alaska still host as many as 35,000? The answer is: Because the ESA originally defined species so that "any subspecies of fish or wildlife or plants, and any distinct population segment of any species..." could also qualify for listing. Otherwise, the fact that peregrine falcons remain in Africa, West Indian manatees in Venezuela, jaguars in Central America, or leatherback sea turtles in the Indian Ocean would be used as an excuse to steamroller across the last ones here at home.

A 1978 amendment to the ESA excluded populations of invertebrates from being listed. Bills now before Congress propose eliminating protection for subspecies and distinct populations of all wildlife. That would include the southern sea otters, California gray whales, bald eagles of the lower 48, American crocodiles, grizzlies, wolves, and a substantial portion of the rest of the threatened and endangered lists.

At first glance, the effort to save the grizzly looks pinned down in a heavy social and political crossfire. Some say it proves that the ESA is too idealistic to serve as a practical conservation tool. Yet research stimulated by the recovery effort shows that the beast we named *horribilis* appears to be learning how to get along in habitats claimed by humans. Grizzlies near the western edge of Glacier Park are feeding and traveling in close proximity to human residences, yet they are doing so mainly at night when they won't be detected, then keeping to thick brush during the day. If they wanted to harm someone, they would have countless opportunities, but the bears are behaving so that most people hardly realize they are around.

Radio-tracking studies just east of the Bob Marshall Wilderness show a similar pattern. The bears travel down out of the tall backcountry onto ranchlands, where they become more nocturnal and secretive. They coexist not only with people but with cows and calves. "I've watched grizzlies move through cattle herds turning over cowpies to get insects and earthworms," Mike Madel, a bear biologist with the Montana Department of Fish, Wildlife and Parks, recalled. "I've even seen cows chase the bears off, and so have other people."

The bears have a bit more trouble resisting sheep, beehives, and orchards. Ranchers are learning to counter the problem simply by placing inexpensive electric fencing around sheep bedding grounds and other easy pickings. A few have started using dogs specially bred and trained to guard against bears. "Depredation on sheep is off by at least 50 percent here," Madel says, "and damage to beehives is down almost 100 percent."

Some female grizzlies are savvy enough about people that they can safely stay in these human-occupied habitats throughout much of the year. This allows them to get at a greater variety of food than they could find up in the mountains. As a result, they are producing cubs at a higher-than-average rate, giving the NCDE population a much-needed boost.

Another intriguing recent discovery is the extent to which other grizzlies in both Yellowstone and the NCDE feed on army cutworm moths during the summer on talus slopes high among the peaks. Huge bears poking around after little insects hardly jibes with the reared-up, snarling pose favored by taxidermists. It makes perfect ecological sense, though, for the moths congregate in fantastic numbers and, pound for pound, contain more protein and fat than fresh steak.

After spending the hottest months at cool elevations, the moths migrate eastward onto the Great Plains, possibly as far as Nebraska, where their eggs develop into larvae and overwinter in the ground. They subsist on plant roots, including those of crops, and farmers spray pesticides to counter the attack. Whether this could affect grizzlies is not yet known, but the relationship between silvertipped bears in the Rockies and grubs wriggling through distant prairie soils illustrates how complex the connections between North American wildlife can be.

Legendary stock killers like Old Three Toes and Old Slaughterhouse might be ashamed of the new breed of grizzly, fleeing from cows and sucking up bugs. But those old-time outlaws had to be awfully cagey in their own right to pull off as many raids as they did while eluding the professional trackers who swore to bring in their hide.

Grizzlies are wonderfully intelligent beings and surprisingly playful even as adults. Some will lie on their back all alone in a meadow to juggle a big log with satisfied roars, or repeatedly slide on their rump down a snowbank chasing rolling chunks of snow. Others, cooling off in a mountain lake during huckleberry time, put their snout underwater

SILVER TROUT
Salvelinus agassizi

————————

Last seen 1930

Native to only two lakes in western New Hampshire, this species perished from overfishing and competition from non-native brook trout.

————————

and exhale, then prick the bubbles with three-inch-long claws. For generations, we gave grizzlies the dimensions of mythical monsters and tried to slay every one we met. The ESA enforced a truce, a breathing space in which each species could get to know the other better. Offered a chance to prove that they could live next to humans, the bears met the challenge. The question is whether we humans can learn to live next to great bears.

More people using grizzly country have come to terms with the fact that they share the space with another smart, adaptable, potentially dangerous mammal, one that likes to eat a lot of the same things we do. Deer hunters and campers are developing the habit of hanging their food high in a tree at night. Cabin owners take better care not to leave garbage around. Timber companies have lately made agreements to protect vital grizzly travel corridors and keep a certain percentage of their lands free of logging disturbance at any given time. Backcountry roads in national forests are closed off to limit travel during critical seasons, and so on.

For all we know, the great bears are nature's way of reminding us to leave room for her to keep working wonders. Ecologists refer to grizzlies as an umbrella species, because taking better care of their habitat automatically provides sufficient habitat for scores of smaller creatures. And it helps ensure clean water, clean air, and open spaces for people. What good are grizzlies? Some folks call them unpredictable, but for others these bears guarantee that there will always be places untouched by what Robert Marshall, the conservationist for whom the Bob Marshall Wilderness is named, described as the "tyrannical impulse of (a mechanized) civilization to conquer every niche on the whole earth." The alternative to blowing away the grizzly is to practice a little humility, which Homo sapiens could always stand to do from time to time. You might even say grizzlies are good for the soul.

They are certainly good for breaking down old mental barriers. The grizzly's situation was one of the earliest examples of a recovery effort that compelled different government agencies to open up new lines of communication. The first steps were taken in the Yellowstone area as land managers realized that the bear population they were supposed to rescue occupied not only the national park but five different national forests, several different Bureau of Land Management districts, various state forests, and private lands in Idaho, Wyoming, and Montana.

Since the bears ignored jurisdictional lines, an Interagency Grizzly Committee was formed to try and look at bear management from the same perspective. In the process, the concept of a greater Yellowstone ecosystem jelled and gained strength. The benefits have carried over to other Yellowstone area inhabitants such as trumpeter swans, cutthroat trout, migratory herds of elk, and, most spectacularly, *Canis lupus,* the endangered gray wolf, reintroduced to the park from Canada in the winter of 1995—further proof that where our last frontiers remain good enough for great bears, they will be good enough for all the other wild things that need homes and space and a little respect.

There are wolves in the NCDE as well. These came down from Canada on their own, reintroducing themselves. In 1979 a female wolf showed up in the North Fork of the Flathead River valley along Glacier Park's western edge. Gray wolves once occupied the whole of the continent but were extirpated in the lower 48 states save for a few score in far northern Minnesota. Under the ESA, the Minnesota wolves have increased to more than 2,000 and expanded into nearby parts of Wisconsin and Michigan. But none had managed to survive for long anywhere else south of Canada in half a century.

SAVE THE WOLVES? That lone gray wolf wasn't the first to probe Montana from the Canadian Rockies. Like her, they usually came alone. A few came in pairs. Most ended up shot or trapped, and the rest wandered on, never to be seen again. This one stuck around. She even got a name: Kishinena, after a bright creek that runs west off the Continental Divide. She was like a ghost, though, shying from roads, turning back if her path so much as cut cross-country ski tracks. And even in midwinter, when she came into heat, nobody ever heard her howl. When a third winter began and found her still alone, it looked as though she might grow old that way. Then researchers lost track of her. But one day in February, a female's prints were found intertwined with those of another wolf. A missing toe on one foot indicated that the newcomer's trip had been a tough one. He died in an accident not long afterward. Yet the next wolf sighting was of seven pups, and they and their mother went on to form what became known as the Magic Pack.

With their range taking in both British Columbia and Montana segments of the North Fork, the pack didn't officially become U.S. wolves until the mid-1980s, when they denned inside Glacier Park for the first time. Despite occasional deaths from poaching, the wolves increased, divided into new groups, and began to disperse into other reaches of the Rockies.

At least seven packs currently roam the NCDE and adjoining lands, most of them descendants of the Magic Pack. One wolf born in Glacier was found 550 miles north in the Yukon Territory. A few have followed the mountains south into central Idaho and into the wildland ecosystem anchored by Yellowstone.

After years of controversy, the government decided to speed up the natural recovery by reintroducing wolves into those areas. The populations were designated "nonessential, experimental," which allows landowners to eliminate wolves that leave the recovery areas and bother livestock. The recovery plan provided that once ten packs are established in each of the two southern ecosystems and the NCDE, the species would be delisted and control over its fate returned to the states, which would manage the wolf as a big game animal.

Public hearings on wolf reintroduction turned out to be even more heated than the debates ignited by grizzly recovery. If anything, the opposition to wolves was so vitriolic that it took a lot of pressure off the bears. There were more than 100 hearings on wolf recovery, and the Fish and Wildlife Service recorded more than 160,000 formal comments. The overwhelming majority of the public, including the citizens of Montana, were in favor of restoring the species. The federal plan moved forward, though groups such as the Farm Bureau and stockmen's associations continued to fight it every step of the way.

As the wolves were being brought from Alberta by plane at the start of 1995, foul winter weather grounded them at a Montana stopover. Opponents won a temporary injunction against the reintroduction, leaving the animals stuck at the airport. Some refused to eat or drink while in their cages and began rapidly losing condition. Then, just as suddenly, the injunction was lifted. Nez Perce Indians arrived to greet the caged wolves and perform ceremonies to welcome them back into the country. The animals went on to establish themselves in Idaho as well as in the Yellowstone ecosystem.

What some count as another success for the ESA is viewed by many stockmen, hunters, and rural Westerners as an example of a law pushed beyond all common sense. A Montana representative to Congress once compared wolves in the backcountry to cockroaches breeding in an attic. Some Wyoming legislators were so incensed by the release of wolves in Yellowstone that they tried to establish a $500 bounty on them. Lawsuits to halt further recovery work are being pressed. Some of the rhetoric harkens all the way back to pioneer days when wolves were reviled as wanton killers and embodiments of evil.

On the opposite side is a new generation of Americans first exposed to wolves on television documentaries, wearing T-shirts

HEATH HEN
Tympanuchus cupido cupido

————————

Last seen 1932

Already decimated from overhunting by the time of the American Revolution, a small population of hens lingered on Martha's Vineyard into the 20th century.

————————

purchased from entire catalogues filled with wolf paraphernalia. They are more likely to revere the wolf as one of nature's crowning achievements—a member of closely knit families that join together in hauntingly beautiful songs. Amid all the competing imagery, it can be hard to know what wolves are truly like in the wild. Current research suggests that wolves given a respite from persecution are, like grizzlies, smart enough to learn how to live around humans with a minimum of conflict.

One pack in the North Fork of the Flathead River valley denned within a quarter-mile of a herd of cows and calves. Another pack regularly used a meadow directly across the river from an even larger herd. Signals from radio-collared wolves revealed them moving past the cattle without incident. Researchers observed the predators ignoring the livestock. Wolves have now lived in the valley for nearly two decades without a single incident of livestock depredation.

Nor is the North Fork unusual in this regard. Another pack established itself across the divide on the same ranchlands visited by grizzlies coming out of the Bob Marshall Wilderness. Cowboys and biologists alike witnessed the wolves resting, playing, and hunting native prey within plain view of grazing cattle. Season after season went by without a problem. Abruptly, a new batch of pups took to killing calves. Two of the young wolves were captured and removed, and the pack continued living quietly on the pasturelands. Similar accounts come from biologists following the other packs in the region.

An environmental group, Defenders of Wildlife, established a fund to compensate ranchers for depredations by wolves, but the 75 to 100 wolves roaming northern Montana in the ongoing natural recovery have killed an average of less than two head of livestock per year. Lightning, accidents, loose dogs, and human vandals kill many hundreds annually. This is not to say that wolves won't gobble up livestock, only that it is not the inevitable outcome of a meeting between wolves and cows. The natural recovery in the Great Lakes region confirms as much. Some 2,000 wolves have been using an area that includes about 7,000 farms. In a typical year, 29 of those farms—less than one-half of one percent—suffer livestock losses. The recent uproar over wolves appears to tell us more about human nature, the strength of cultural traditions, and our limitless capacity for demonizing perceived enemies than about the nature of wolves.

The concern that wolves would tear into the wild hoofed herds and keep increasing until they had all but wiped out deer, elk, and other big game has proved equally unfounded. As the wolves were expanding in the North Fork, game populations increased to their highest level in recent memory. The abundance of wild prey helps explain the wolves' limited interest in livestock and, conversely, why wolves became such notorious livestock-raiders during the settlement era, when their natural food supply was at an all-time low. We had just eliminated the bison. Elk and pronghorn would have been listed as threatened had there been an ESA, and even the ubiquitous deer had become rare in the face of unchecked commercial and subsistence shooting. Yet it was the wolves that got labeled greedy.

The North Fork wolves multiplied until they numbered between 25 and 40 in the late 1980s. Dividing the valley among two or three packs, they have maintained those numbers ever since, because competition for territories and mates keeps forcing a percentage of the wolves to emigrate.

As a rule, only the alpha male and female in a pack breed, and the pack as a whole vigorously defends its territory against incursions by neighbors. Within Alaska's Denali National Park, where wolves have been studied for almost half a century, fighting with other wolves is the main cause of death. Such aggression is a common means by which predators at the top of the food chain keep from becoming overpopu-

lated in relation to their food supply. As the most widespread and efficient social predator in North America, wolves played a crucial role in honing the very qualities we admire in hooved wildlife, from the fleetness of antelope to the mountain goat's climbing skills. Over the long run, the packs are creators, not destroyers.

For that matter, wolves were the raw material from which the well-loved companions we know as dogs were formed. The two kinds of canine are still virtually the same species genetically. All of our pets and livestock are offshoots of wildlife, and in the debates over saving species we might do well to pause and consider which ones could one day give rise to other domestic animals.

The fascinating thing about the North Fork these days is that there is not just one major carnivore present but three: wolves, grizzlies, and mountain lions, or cougars, all competing for moose, elk, mule deer, and whitetailed deer. Wolves and cougars are pure hunters. The wolves seem to concentrate on deer, while the cougars focus more on elk at times. Some idealistic supporters of wildlife believe that such predators mainly target old, sick, or injured prey, helping keep herds healthy by culling the least fit members. That is only partly true. Predators take whichever herd members are easiest to get. While those do include the old and infirm, they generally include even more of the very young. Under certain conditions, such as on ice or in deep, crusted snows that cause hooved animals to flounder, the hunters are quite capable of killing even the healthiest specimens, and do.

In a way, grizzlies are the biggest opportunists of all, being hunters, scavengers, or vegetarians, depending on individual predilections and what is available at the moment. Some North Fork grizzlies prey heavily on moose during the birthing season, using their extraordinary sense of smell to locate the newborn calves. Taking advantage of ungulates wounded or killed by sportsmen during the fall hunting season, a few large males developed a pattern of staying afield well into

December, long after females and their cubs had retreated to winter dens. Recently, with wolves back in the thick of things and mountain lion numbers having built up along with the ungulate populations, some grizzlies are remaining active right on through the winter. They are following the wolf packs and, especially, the lions to take over their kills.

This may be unusual or it may be perfectly natural. We don't know. Modern wildlife biologists never had a chance to study a full complement of Rocky Mountain species before. Bears on Kodiak Island sometimes stay awake through mild winters to feed on late runs of salmon, roots, and leftover berries. Grizzlies don't truly hibernate, as black bears do. The silvertips merely take an extended snooze, from which they can awaken at any time. With their bulk and insulating fur, they have no particular need to hide from winter as long as they can keep finding nourishment.

Having wolf and cougar kills to scavenge could prove a boon to grizzly survival. On the other hand, wolves have been seen attacking grizzly cubs in the North Fork. Wolves have also killed young cougars. "African lions will home in on circling vultures and go take over a cheetah's meal," Diane Boyd, a University of Montana researcher, revealed. "Here the wolves scan the sky for ravens and bald eagles, and it looks like the packs might be chasing cougars off a fair number of fresh kills."

Studies by University of Montana researchers show that the North Fork's hoofed herds have begun to decline from their peak levels over the past several years due in part to predation. Overall, the kill is fairly evenly divided among the wolves, cougars, grizzlies, and human hunters. Where will the trends lead from here? Will a balance be struck at a certain level or will the community fluctuate in dynamic ways we never even considered before? We will know only as the story continues to unfold. Because a long-silent female wolf met a three-toed male in a

WABASH RIFFLESHELL
epioblasma sampsonii

————

Last seen 1900s

Dams, pollution, and siltation combined to destroy the habitat of this freshwater mussel, one of nearly two dozen mussel species to vanish in the past 50 years.

————

time when the law was on their side, the meaning of wild has expanded for this part of the world. Because the ESA halted the grizzly's rapid downward slide, you don't have to go to Africa to find a pageant of big beasts interacting with one another.

In Yellowstone, where coyotes were plentiful and tended to become bold panhandlers along park roads, wolves have killed some, chased off others, and appear to be drastically rearranging the smaller canines' niche in that ecosystem. The wolves may ease the chronic overcrowding of elk on Yellowstone ranges. One certain change is that the wolves have become one of the park's most popular tourist attractions. A study by John Duffield, an economist at the University of Montana, estimates that the wolves' drawing power could add at least five million dollars annually to the Yellowstone area's economy, 40 percent of which is based upon tourism.

The continent's smaller wolf species—*Canis rufus,* the red wolf, native to the Southeast—was persecuted until the 45- to 80-pound predators began to mate with coyotes for want of their own kind. The Fish and Wildlife Service took in the last holdouts for captive breeding just in time: Only 17 true red wolves stood between the species and extinction. "We've got more than 60 back out in the wild now," Gary Henry, the recovery coordinator, said, observing an adult male lope through its new range in North Carolina's 150,000-acre Alligator River National Wildlife Refuge. "As they move out from here, it's no longer biology but human attitudes that count."

And, predictably, there is resistance to the recovery in neighboring rural areas. The red wolves have been blamed for the deaths of chickens and goats that turned out to be the work of marauding dogs, and one county politician believes that children will no longer be safe playing outdoors.

Nevertheless, we have come a long way. In 1905 Montana passed a law forcing veterinarians to infect captured wolves with the scabies mites that cause sarcoptic mange, a debilitating condition characterized by widespread hair loss and skin infections, then turn them loose to contaminate surviving wild packs. Bounty hunters spread traps and predator poisons at will. Government hunters took over after them. Working for the Animal Damage Control division of the Fish and Wildlife Service, their job was to track down and exterminate every last wolf and grizzly, no matter how long it took.

Wolves were our most direct competitors for meat throughout the northern hemisphere not long ago. Today, we are willing to carry them in our trucks and planes and even in our arms to a place where their kind can thrive. The Fish and Wildlife Service is looking into the possibility of reintroducing the Mexican wolf, *Canis lupus baileyi*, from captive breeding facilities to its native range in New Mexico and perhaps Arizona.

Grizzlies can rip humans to pieces. Yet we find ourselves able to admire them and are at work to make sure that they, too, have a place in the sun. The Fish and Wildlife Service has proposed transplanting grizzlies into the Selway-Bitterroot wilderness ecosystem that includes central Idaho and portions of western Montana. The hope is that having a third major Lower 48 population in addition to the NCDE and Yellowstone would offer the species enough security that the agency could delist it. The reaction among people living near that wilderness has been mixed—a marked improvement from the way rural Westerners felt about grizzly recovery when it got under way more than two decades ago. Injuries to hikers from grizzlies in Glacier Park are extremely uncommon, and a couple of the people who have been hurt said to the rangers taking them out to get medical help that they realized they were intruders in the great bears' domain and hoped the bears wouldn't be killed as a result of the incident.

In discussing endangered species issues, we have a tendency to dwell on the conflicts involved. Considering where our grandparents started, however, the fact that these are issues at all speaks of amazing progress. Even as the ESA illuminates the difficulties of figuring out how to live together with other creatures, it shines a still brighter light on the tolerance and hope at work in this land.

GRIZZLY BEAR

By the 1920s every specimen of *Ursus arctos horribilis* had disappeared from California, most of them hunted down like this one in 1887. The grizzly bear now exists only in Washington, Idaho, Montana, and Wyoming—and in Alaska where the population is still abundant.

2

....

The Little Pieces

IF YOU REALLY WANT TO UNDERSTAND ECOLOGY, YOU might want to start carrying a pocket magnifying glass. Most wildlife is small; the average length for animal species is well under half an inch. Though easy to overlook, the diminutive creatures generally play more essential roles in the functioning of ecosystems than large creatures do. The very existence of most big life-forms rests upon legions of smaller ones. Aldo Leopold, the naturalist whose writings during the first half of this century helped formulate an American conservation ethic, called these smaller species the little cogs and wheels that run the world.

"We like to think we are living in the Age of Man," Mike Ivie, an internationally known entomologist, remarked, "but we are obviously living in the Age of Beetles." Insects make up 80 percent of all the species identified so far, and one out of every three insect species—therefore, about one of every four known species on earth—is a beetle. Biologists often quote J.B.S. Haldane, a renowned British physiologist and philosopher, who, when asked what he had learned of God through his scientific studies, replied that the Creator must have "an inordinate fondness for beetles." The American burying beetle, *Nicrophorus americanus*, almost qualifies as charismatic megafauna. Up to one-and-a-half inches long, it carries a bold pattern of orange-red splotches on its dark body and sports bright orange tips on its clublike antennae. Its behavior includes a level of parental care more typical of warm-blooded vertebrates than of six-legged beasts.

Like scavenging bears and bald eagles, burying beetles feed on the bodies of dead animals. Detecting the odor of decay from as far away as a mile or two, they fly to the carcass and produce a scent of their own, a pheremone, to attract a mate. The two often do battle with other burying beetles until just one pair is left in possession of the carcass, usually that of a fair-size bird or modest-size mammal. The male and female then set about burying the carcass six to eight inches deep, excavating the soil directly below it. Where the ground is hard or rocky, the beetles may lie on their back underneath the carcass and, in a coordinated effort, raise it with their legs and push it along to softer ground. They are known to lift animals 200 times their own weight and move them for several feet this way.

The beetles use their jaws to clip away feathers or fur. Then they coat the skin with secretions that seal the flesh and inhibit the growth of bacteria and fungi, ensuring that the food supply won't decompose too quickly. The beetles gradually fold the body into a ball during burial. Finally, they excavate a tunnel that leads from the carcass to a brood chamber in which the female lays her eggs.

Six days later, the eggs hatch into larvae, and the parents begin bringing them food from the carcass. The young beetles rear up and "beg" to be fed, stroking the jaws of the adult somewhat like wolf pups do to stimulate an older pack member to regurgitate a meal of meat. (In the closely related carrion beetle genus *Silpha*, the larvae not only "beg" but chirrup like baby birds by rubbing a comblike structure on the outside of

THISMIA AMERICANUS
(no common name)

———

Last seen 1912

The only samples of this flower were collected in 1912, in an area of Chicago that is now an industrial site. Its closest relatives exist in New Zealand and Tasmania.

———

their body.) While the female burying beetle does most of the feeding, the male stays to guard the brood against invaders and help remove mold from the carcass. After about two weeks of growth, the larvae disperse into the soil to pupate, emerging as adults 48 to 60 days afterward.

In the early part of the century, the burying beetle was found in almost three dozen states and parts of Canada. By the time the species was listed as endangered, in 1989, scientists could locate only several hundred of the insects on Block Island, off the coast of Rhode Island, and a few more in one Oklahoma county.

TWO CATEGORIES OF SPECIES are particularly vulnerable to extinction. The first are those with specialized niches. Examples from the endangered list would be the Everglade snail kite, which feeds almost exclusively on apple snails; the Devils Hole pupfish, confined to isolated springs within the Mojave desert; and the San Diego mesa-mint of California's coastal sage scrub community. As a particular habitat or food supply dwindles, so does the species.

The second type of creatures at risk are those with low rates of reproduction. Generally long-lived, they have small batches of offspring and, in the case of animals, invest a large amount of time and effort rearing their young to maturity. Examples would be the whooping crane and bald eagle; the California condor, which typically lays one or, at most, two eggs every other year; the grizzly bear, which does not breed before five to seven years of age and gives birth every three years on average; and the threatened western prairie fringed orchid, which may wait ten years before it first blossoms and thereafter flowers only at intervals of several years.

Within a given group of animals, the largest species tend to have the lowest reproductive rates, and this relationship holds among bury-ing beetles. North America has 15 species of *Nicrophorus,* and *americanus* is the biggest. The 3 to 35 eggs the female lays are an extremely small number by insect standards, while the development period is long compared to that of flies or mosquitoes, which can quickly multiply into millions under ideal conditions. Perhaps it is not so surprising, then, that the American burying beetle has become imperiled. The surprise is that we should choose to grant the same sort of protection to a beetle—especially one whose habits earned it the common name of gravedigger—as we extend to a great bear or a whale.

Exactly what triggered the American burying beetle's dramatic decline is a mystery. Pesticides would seem an obvious culprit, but the population apparently began to collapse before chemicals were in widespread use. Scientists speculate that the species' demise might be an aftershock from the extinction of the passenger pigeon.

The heaviest natural losses in birds occur among the young, and young passenger pigeons were exactly the size of animal that burying beetles seem to favor. Though no accurate tally of passenger pigeons was ever made, their numbers may have matched or exceeded those of all the other birds on the continent combined. John James Audubon, the early 19th-century artist and naturalist, estimated one passing flock to hold more than a billion pigeons. "The light of noon-day was obscured as by an eclipse," he wrote. Alexander Wilson, a highly regarded ornithologist, recorded another flock of more than two billion in 1810. Settlers slaughtered the birds wholesale at their roosts. Farmers set fire to trees in the enormous colonial nesting areas and brought in hogs to feed on the scorched young that littered the ground.

A perfect symbol of the New World's seemingly limitless bounty, the passenger pigeon became extinct on September 1, 1914, when the last one died alone in a cage at the Cincinnati Zoo. The last Carolina parakeet perished in the same place February 21, 1918, though women still strolled about wearing the blue, red, and green wings of the colorful parakeets pinned to hats that would soon go out of fashion. Prairie chickens became rare across the Great Plains, and the form previously common in the East, the heath hen, went the way of the passenger pigeon. All that biomass was suddenly gone from the beetles' larder.

The main reason beetles bury a carcass is to keep it away from competitors. Once *americanus's* primary sources of food became scarce, it may have been at a disadvantage competing against carrion beetles better able to use smaller carcasses. At the same time, changes caused by logging, ranching, and farming led to an increase in mid-size vertebrates that also competed for carcasses: scavenging magpies and crows, plus the skunks and raccoons no longer kept in check by big carnivores such as wolves. Research in the tropics has shown that habitat fragmentation removes the larger species of carrion beetles and dung beetles from an ecosystem first, just as the first to go among the vertebrates tend to be the big mammals and birds.

Then again, the American burying beetle could have been the victim of a new pathogen introduced from abroad or of some entirely natural calamity. Why should Rhode Island's Block Island have remained one of its strongholds? Because it is isolated. And because Elizabeth Dickens once shot a swan there. It was a black swan, native to Australia, that had somehow wandered off course. The incident kindled her abiding interest in ornithology, and she passed along that sense of wonder to Block Island schoolchildren for the next several decades.

"Elizabeth Dickens would come into school once a month and give lectures on birds," Captain Robert Lewis, a retired Navy officer who lives on Block Island, remembered. "Kids kept bird lists to read off when she called on them. We would bring any dead bird we found to Miss Dickens, and she would somehow find the money to have it mounted as a specimen. Another prominent citizen, Earl Dodge, got us interested in planting trees, as the island was bare from farming and grazing. So you see, we've all been educated to take care of our island. It was quite natural to be alarmed when the developers started coming in."

Visited by as many as 15,000 tourists a weekend during summer, Block Island was a prime candidate for large-scale vacation home development. But islanders are perhaps more keenly aware of limits than are mainland dwellers. Led by Captain Lewis and others, the Block Islanders formed an association that began buying up and setting aside country acreage slated for subdivision. The state and federal governments provided matching dollars. A privately funded national group, the Nature Conservancy, joined in, making Block Island one of its top priorities for ecosystem protection in the Western Hemisphere.

Robert Lewis, his brother, Bill, and Robert's son, Keith, have all donated land of their own, portions of a farm that had been in the family since 1817. In the 1970s, only 100 of the island's 6,460 acres were publicly owned. Today, nearly one in every four acres has been preserved for the community as open space.

Block Island is one of the top areas for birding on the East Coast. In addition to serving as a key stopover for migrants, it has become a refuge for birds no longer seen anywhere else in the state; among them, the northern harrier, American bittern, grasshopper sparrow, and upland plover. Like most states, Rhode Island has its own list of species threatened or endangered within its borders. Five of the state-listed plants now exist only on Block Island, along with the indigenous Block Island vole. Since the island was never sprayed with DDT, it also holds a variety of moths and butterflies now rare on the mainland.

Block Island's fields and woodlands support some of the densest pheasant and woodcock populations known. This provides the American burying beetles with plenty of carcasses of the size they prefer. An absence of mammalian predators benefits the birds and may have proved a boon to the beetles as well.

One recent June morning, a crew of biologists and volunteers went to check a series of pitfall traps baited with rotting meat, a technique that helps them keep track of *americanus* numbers. Their course led across an old family farm donated to the community by Elizabeth Dickens. They found five American burying beetles in the first trap and nine in another, a marked improvement over the previous day, when the biologists had seen so few that they began nervously joking about a crash in the population. The next trap was at the corner of an old rock wall in a hayfield ringed by wild viburnum and bayberry. It held a beetle that had been captured and marked with pigment the previous day half a mile away in Rodman's Hollow, pastureland that Block Island citizens bought back from speculators.

"Hey, here's an *orbicollis*," exclaimed the sharpest-eyed naturalist in the group, 4-year-old John Raithel, homing in on a smaller burying beetle species, "and—look!—another *americanus*." John's father, Chris Raithel, of the Rhode Island Fish and Game Department, pointed out mites clustered in the hollows and crevices of the endangered insect. Hitching rides on big beetles is a way to avoid predators and also allows the wingless mites to disperse. In return, they eat fly eggs and microbes, helping clean both the beetle and the buried carcass it tends. As many as 14 species of mites from four separate taxonomic families associate with the American burying beetle. Some may depend on *americanus* to the extent that they would be bound to follow it into extinction.

After marking the beetles, the researchers covered the traps so no other animals could fall in, then set the captives free. Before flying, the beetles climbed to the highest nearby point, usually a scientist's head or an upheld arm. As one prepared for take-off, it carefully cleaned its multifaceted eyes and orange-tipped antennae with catlike

DUSKY SEASIDE SPARROW
Ammodranus maritimus mirabilis

————

Last seen 1987

Construction of the Kennedy Space Center and subsequent development of Florida's St. Johns River valley destroyed too much of the sparrow's habitat for it to survive.

————

strokes of the forelegs, which held a brush of hairs. Next, it swiveled its head back and forth, getting a fix on the sun, a faint scent, or some kaleidoscopic image of the landscape we can only imagine.

In some ways the American burying beetle is as different from us as any movie screen alien. Yet the insect is more beautiful, far more intricate, and, in the end, built of the same firing nerves, contracting muscles, and flowing chemical broths that animate our closer relatives within the animal kingdom. Fine pits and grooves pattern the elytra, the protective anterior wings that covers a beetle's back—part of the armor contributing to their extraordinary success as a group. Poised at the tip of a researcher's fingertip, a beetle lifted those elytra, exposing delicate, amber wings. They unfolded and began whirring noisily until the animal rose like a bulky helicopter churning away into the morning air and an unknown future.

Counts on Block Island are slightly down over the past few years. But a captive population established at the Cincinnati Zoo Insectarium has multiplied to several hundred. A second captive population under the care of entomologist Andrea Kozol produced animals that were transplanted to Penikese Island, off the Massachusetts coast. After the beetles showed signs of surviving and reproducing there, the Fish and Wildlife Service transplanted another group to Nantucket Island.

West of the Mississippi, only 33 of the insects were located between 1980 and 1989. The subsequent listing of *americanus* prompted searches that brought a welcome surprise: burying beetles turned up in more than a dozen different Oklahoma counties and four more counties in neighboring Arkansas. A wildlife manager in Nebraska noticed a couple of American burying beetles when he lifted a boat overturned on the ground. Another beetle was discovered mounted on a pin in an eight-year-old girl's insect collection on display at a county fair in northern Nebraska. Live ones were then found in that area and two adjoining South Dakota counties.

The increase in the beetle's numbers reflects the fact that more people are looking harder for them. The ESA requires people to check for American burying beetles before proceeding with activities that would alter habitats in or near places where the species is known to exist. If beetles are located, Section 7 dictates that no federally funded project can proceed until the agency involved consults with the Fish and Wildlife Service about ways to mitigate possible effects on the insect's population.

Of a thousand endangered species consultations in Oklahoma during 1992, fully one quarter involved the American burying beetle. Construction of a highway and gas line were halted in Oklahoma, and expansion of a landfill near Fort Smith, Arkansas, was put on hold. As the beetles appeared in more sites, they were less likely to be in jeopardy from any one project. Consequently, work was allowed to proceed as usual, with the simple stipulation that any *americanus* in the immediate area be relocated to safer spots.

Is prospecting for big, orange-spotted beetles and carrying them out of harm's way too much to ask? Some would answer: Absolutely; the ESA was supposed to secure a future for the likes of Steller sea lions and Florida's Key deer, not slow down business because of some creepy-crawler in the neighborhood. What possible reason do we have for trying to save a burying beetle?

"This insect focused attention on the issue of land development in a dramatic way," remarked Dennis Wolkoff, vice president of the Nature Conservancy Block Island chapter. "It helped bring together people who want to save the island's character with people working on the science end of conservation." Michael Amaral, a Fish and Wildlife Service biologist, observed, "If biodiversity is going to be more than a fancy word, we have to get serious about paying attention to the little creatures. On a practical level, burying beetles reduce the carrion available to ants and flies, which could otherwise reach pest proportions. The beetles also eat the flies' larvae. Like dung beetles, they are an important link in cycles of decomposition and nutrient recycling."

Like Block Island, Martha's Vineyard, off the Massachusetts coast, preserved a fair amount of open space and has come to serve as a stronghold for an array of creatures now either rare or absent on the mainland. One is the northeastern beach tiger beetle, endangered because it lives on the same sandy shores that hordes of humans love to walk and drive along. Vehicles are particularly destructive because they pack down the loose sand, crushing larvae and the beetles' tunnel systems.

Wildlife officials have been trying to address the problem. When stretches of shoreline were closed off to the public, though, it was done in the name of beach-nesting birds. This was perfectly legitimate, as the threatened piping plover and endangered least tern use the same areas the beetles do. Both birds have been hard hit by human disturbance, and their nesting success improves markedly on beaches where foot and motor traffic are controlled. Enough fishermen and dune buggy enthusiasts were raising a ruckus about feathered animals cutting into their recreation that the biologists were not about to confront them with an endangered beetle subspecies.

Attitudes, like types of wildlife, vary from place to place. The banks of the Connecticut River in New Hampshire support another endangered subspecies of tiger beetle, a fast-flying, colorful hunter called the Puritan tiger. Shops in the nearby town of Plainfield sell T-shirts sporting the beetle's image. The citizens have made the fact that the creature still finds a home near them a source of civic pride, and they even sponsor an annual Puritan tiger festival.

AS DIRECTOR OF THE RIVERSIDE COUNTY (California) Habitat Conservation Agency, Brian Loew is obliged to save the Stephens' kangaroo rat, an endangered, long-tailed, hopping rodent whose arid grassland and chaparral habitat has become the backyards of homes in new housing subdivisions. "You don't know the real ESA until you deal with mom and pop who want to put in a trailer they've saved for all their lives, and you tell them they might have to change their plans because of a 'rat,'" he cautioned. "I've come home to death threats on my answering machine."

Some homeowners wanted to replace the native plants with lawn. They were told they could not alter habitat critical to the kangaroo rat. When the owners cited possible danger from brush fires, the Fish and Wildlife Service sought a compromise, permitting people to mow the natural vegetation as long as they didn't destroy it by tearing out the roots. Blazes often do sweep these hills; in fact, the chaparral community is naturally adapted to, and maintained by, wildfire. In 1993, flames raged through the area and took out several trailer homes. Officials maintained that the fire was driven by such strong Santa Ana winds that it would have claimed the homes no matter what was growing in the yard. The landowners didn't see it that way, Loew explained. They blamed the "rat" and the "feds" for making them homeless. The incident aggravated an already bitter controversy and became an oft-repeated horror story among property rights activists working to roll back the ESA.

"We also have the Delhi Sands flower-loving fly," Loew said, referring to the ESA's first protected fly, listed in 1993. "It's on the border of Riverside and San Bernadino Counties in a beat-up, weedy spot set aside as an enterprise zone with tax incentives for industrial development. So here we go, trying with all our might to save rats and flies in an

ALANI
Mellicope balloui

———

Last seen 1927

Though believed to be extinct, this plant was listed in 1994 to protect any specimens that may reappear.

———

area of high unemployment. What a thankless job. Some of the hard feelings stem from the fact that a few environmentalists use the ESA just to fend off developments they don't like. Got a problem with the mall proposed next door? Go out and find a rare species there. If they're not careful, they're going to undermine support for what has become the strongest land-use law in the nation."

As numerous as insects are, and as rudimentary as our knowledge of this vast class is, we have little idea of the number on the verge of disappearing. The answer might turn out to be tens of thousands. If all were listed and the ESA's provisions enforced, the outcome would probably not be the rescue of hard-pressed species but a political backlash against the act beyond anything seen so far.

The first insect species wasn't listed until 1985. Relatively few have been added since. Invertebrates as a whole remain a minority on the list, though they comprise the overwhelming majority of animal life. This isn't just because small creatures tend to be less popular with the public or because wildlife experts fear a backlash. It is also because there are no guidelines that address how far down the scale of life it is practical to list species.

Florida is home to an endangered lichen, Florida perforate cladonia. It is a lovely, lacey, lime-gold ground-dweller, and it is important to the Florida oak scrub ecosystem because it colonizes recently burned areas and helps hold the soil, initiating the process of building a new organic layer in which other plants can establish themselves. Lichens can also be valuable indicators of air quality, as they are especially sensitive to pollution. Yet a lichen is not a single organism but a symbiotic mixture of a fungus and a type of cyanobacteria, formerly called blue-green algae. Should we save individual bacteria species, when several thousand can be found in a teaspoon of typical soil?

How do we answer the riddle of what to do about the last small-pox? Estimated to have claimed 2 million human lives as recently as 1967, the virus was eradicated in the human population a decade later. The only cultures in existence are carefully stored at a select handful of laboratories. What if an earthquake or human error allowed some to escape into a populace no longer immune to the disease? Should we get rid of them now? What if a similar disease broke out somewhere on the globe and the cure lay in studying the only smallpox left or in genetically engineering a new vaccine from it?

No society has ever confronted such choices before. No society has ever known enough to judge other species, and we may not either. Perhaps the best we can do is muddle ahead with whatever seems reasonable at the time, keeping two things uppermost in our minds: One, the definition of "reasonable" may change drastically as we uncover new information; and, two, there is no going back from a decision that renders a creature extinct.

THE GROUP OF ANIMALS MOST AT RISK in our country is also one of the least conspicuous: freshwater mussels. The U.S. has the greatest variety of these mollusks in the world, 297 different species in all, concentrated mainly in the Southeast. At last count, 57 were listed as threatened or endangered, 74 were seriously declining, and at least 20 are presumed extinct. Does this truly matter? What good is a fine-rayed pigtoe anyway?

"Shiny pigtoe," Dick Neves shouted, holding two fist-size mussels aloft as he burst from the cool waters of Virginia's Clinch River, "and a fine-rayed pigtoe, both endangered." A mollusk expert with the National Biological Services, Neves was snorkeling around Pendleton Island, a mussel stronghold purchased a decade ago by the Nature Conservancy.

He submerged again and was soon hovering above a pocketbook mussel whose mantle has an outgrowth that mimics a tiny fish, complete with eyespots and finny tail. This tissue pulses rhythmically so that the "fish" looks as if it were actually swimming. When a real fish rushes in to gulp the lure, the mussel releases a burst of microscopic larvae that clamp onto the fish's gills. After hitchhiking awhile like mites on a burying beetle, they drop off and begin life on the bottom. Which is how animals that seldom move keep replenishing their population upstream against the current.

Freshly opened shells along the riverbank attested that mussels are a food source for raccoons, muskrats, wading birds such as herons, and waterfowl. They feed otters and strong-jawed fish as well, while a variety of smaller fish use the old shells as shelters and egg-laying sites.

Another name for freshwater mussels is pearlymussels. Their lustrous inner shells kept as many as 150 factories busy producing most of the buttons manufactured in America until the 1940s, when plastic began to take over. Today the U.S. annually sells Japan and other nations some 50 million dollars' worth of the shells from certain large, common varieties residing in large rivers. They make the best beads for stimulating oysters to form pearls. For that matter, freshwater mussels can produce the odd pearl themselves.

Some consider the argument that you never know which humble organism will hold the cure for cancer a conservationist's ploy for extending ESA protections, but freshwater mussels happen to be notably resistant to tumors and are the subject of medical research. The canary-in-the-coal-mine rationale for saving wildlife also fits mussels especially well. Being filter-feeders, freshwater mussels play important roles in keeping water clean within a river system; that is, they do for free a chore that would otherwise cost untold millions. At the same time, straining sediment and algae at the very bottom of the food chain makes mussels highly sensitive indicators of pollution.

The endangered list holds far more aquatic animals than land-dwelling ones to begin with, because almost everything a society produces sooner or later ends up in the creek. The mollusks, some of which live a century, accumulate toxins from pesticides, waste treatment plants, chemical spills, household cleaners flushed down drains, and chemicals sprayed on lawns. Mussels downstream from coal mines are dying from acid runoff and concentrations of heavy metals. They get buried by sediments from strip mining, dredging, intensive agriculture, and overuse of streambanks by livestock. Those adapted to fast-moving water, as most are, vanish when dams turn rivers into series of lakes. They dwindle as all these pressures also take out the fish that act as hosts to young mussels. And now they face the zebra mussel, a stowaway from the Black, Caspian, and Azov Seas. Like kudzu, fire ants, and many other exotics—the U.S. is contending with at least 4,500 alien species at the moment—the zebra is multiplying unchecked by natural enemies, smothering native mussel beds as it spreads.

A DISPROPORTIONATE NUMBER OF THE INSECTS listed as threatened or endangered in the U.S. are butterflies. Not that this group is in the worst shape; they just happen to be beautiful, relatively well studied, and blessed with more supporters than other insects. Lepidopterists have long prized tropical Morpho butterflies for their wings of shimmering blue. This iridescent color is not from pigment. The wing scales are actually transparent. Microscopic ridges on them reflect light waves in patterns that cancel out other colors while reinforcing blue. How a wing scale cell constructs such elaborate texturing is the subject of intense research these days. A Japanese team has had some success trying to duplicate the structure with inorganic materials. The hope is to eventually apply knowledge gained from butterfly wings to the

HAU KUAHIWI
Hibiscadelphus crucibracteatus

————

Last seen 1985

The only known specimen of this tree was discovered in 1981 on the Hawaiian island of Lana'i and died four years later. All attempts to grow seeds from the tree failed.

production of new types of coatings, filters, and diffraction grates for optical equipment; storage materials for the communications and information industries, which increasingly employ fiber optics; and selective solar absorbers for the energy industry.

Queen Alexandra's birdwing butterfly of New Guinea and the Luzon peacock swallowtail butterfly of the Philippines are among the foreign species listed under the ESA. The list of imperiled U.S. species includes the Karner blue, El Segundo blue, Palos Verde blue, Smith's blue, lotis blue, and mission blue butterflies. Although they don't necessarily create their coruscating colors the same way as Morpho species, their own methods may yield products with equal promise.

"Many of us… have perhaps unconsciously assumed that small things must be simple," Helen Ghiradella, studying the structural colors of butterflies at State University in New York, told *Science News*. "This may not be the case; and indeed, the further we investigate, the more complexity we seem to find." For the scientist, as for the poet, there are as many levels of wonder in the silent beat of a butterfly wing as in the howl of a wolf.

How many things do we wear that are blue? Another reason scientists want to copy the natural magic of the butterfly is to devise alternative ways of giving hues to everyday materials; the blue in clothing and plastics is currently achieved with dyes and coloring agents that often contain poisonous compounds that even at lower concentrations can cause allergic reactions.

While latex from the Brazilian rubber plant has been a gift of incalculable value to modern civilization, 17 million people in the U.S. alone are allergic to it. Their reactions may be as mild as an itch or as potentially deadly as systemic shock. Yet society can hardly do without rubber gloves, catheters, and condoms these days. A synthetic latex that is nonallergenic exists, but a stronger, more elastic version has lately been derived from the desert shrub called guayule—*Parthenium argentatum*, native to the American Southwest. According to Agriculture Department scientists who developed the product, guayule latex, unlike its synthetic counterpart, is also impermeable to viruses. Guayule is not imperiled at the moment, but it stands as an obvious reminder of why little-known species can be worth taking care of.

Although purple coneflower of America's heartland, *Echinacea angustifolia*, is not considered imperiled either, the native prairie to which it belongs has become alarmingly scarce. Plains Indian shamans would rub purple coneflower root extract on their hands, then walk through camp lifting boiling meat out of pots to impress everybody. Theatrics aside, this member of the sunflower and daisy family was used by many tribes to treat ailments from ordinary colds to snakebite. In laboratory tests *Echinacea* does show anesthetic, anti-inflammatory, and antibiotic properties and increases the resistance of cell cultures to viruses, including flu and herpes. One compound it produces appears to stimulate the immune system. *Echinacea tenneseensis*, Tennessee purple coneflower, and *Echinacea laevigata*, smooth coneflower, both native to the eastern U.S., are on the endangered list, in part because too many folks have been picking them to sell. *Echinacea* extracts are in increasing demand at health stores. Gardeners like coneflowers for their ornamental value, and some species produce a natural insecticide.

Even leeches are getting a second look from the medical community. They may be blood-suckers, but at least they do it painlessly using a natural anesthetic, hyaluronidase. Because the enzyme is also an anticoagulant, doctors have found that putting leeches on patients can help relieve the build-up of blood pressure after some types of operations, notably microsurgery to attach severed body parts.

The more closely we look into nature, the less farfetched seems the claim that any one of the creatures around us could provide the next major advance in food, fiber, or medicine—including a new weapon against cancer. It is a straightforward statistical probability. A number of obscure species such as the tropical rosy periwinkle, effective in the treatment of leukemia, are already actively employed as anti-cancer agents. Half of the pharmaceutical products in current use were derived from wild species around the globe, most them unfamiliar to the general public. Encoded within the genes of these organisms are millions of years' worth of solutions to the question of how to live on this planet. To discard even one species before its time could be tragically shortsighted. This is the parable of the Biblical ark, and it is more relevant than ever today because we are on the verge of understanding so much, aided by technologies whose powers are increasing by quantum leaps yearly.

Recently, Jane Shen-Miller, of the University of California at Los Angeles, filed through the hard outer shell of a lotus seed from China and soaked it in water. Four days later it was growing, which wouldn't have been unusual if this seed had not been formed during the T'ang dynasty and lain dormant for the next 1,288 years. Believed to be the oldest vascular plant ever revived, the species must have a powerful genetic blueprint to delay aging, and researchers are now hard at work trying to read it. Yet what is a mere 1,288 years to the bacteria that spent tens of thousands of years preserved in the stomach of a mammoth and started multiplying again as soon as modern paleontologists unearthed the Ice Age mammal?

The question of how long the spark of life can be stored also concerns freshwater mollusk specialist Dick Neves. "We're simply going to have to write off some mussel species and try to get the others through this spasm of extinction any way we can," he remarked in his lab, where he is testing methods for freezing the larvae into a state of suspended animation. Perhaps there, in vats of liquid nitrogen, they can hold on until they have clean, flowing rivers to live in again.

IN **1971** A CITIZENS GROUP SUED to stop construction of the Tellico Dam on the Little Tennessee River. "Tellico was a classic boondoggle," Dave Etnier, an icthyologist at the University of Tennessee, asserted. "The costs of building it far outweighed the projected revenues." In addition to prime farmland and family homes, society stood to lose the river bottom area called *Tanasi* (Tennessee), sacred core of the old Cherokee Nation. Speculators who had bought up future lakefront property appeared to be the main beneficiaries. The citizens' lawsuit was unsuccessful.

Etnier reached down while snorkeling one day and lifted an unfamiliar, three-inch-long, bottom-scooting fish up into the light. He named it the snail darter. Eating mainly snails—another type of freshwater mollusk—it made its home on shoals around the Tellico area and apparently nowhere else. Then the ESA passed, and *Percina tanasi* was soon listed as endangered. A court halted work on the nearly completed dam, and all at once the whole country was talking about the ESA.

Some marveled that this new law really had the teeth to shut down a project with ten years of labor and 100 million dollars invested in it. Others, including some in Congress, were aghast. Had we really passed a bill that would allow some small, unfamiliar fish to halt the march of progress? The snail darter was ridiculed until, for many, it became a standing joke. The Cherokee wouldn't have laughed. Their creation myths celebrate the small and drab among the animal people. They say it was Beaver's grandchild, Water Beetle, who dove down beneath the waves that once covered the world and brought up the scoop of mud that grew to become the land we live upon, and Water Spider who first captured fire, carrying a live coal from a lightning-struck tree in the silken bowl she had spun upon her back.

FRANKLINIA TREE
Franklinia alatahama

————

Last seen in wild, 1790

Named for Benjamin Franklin, this tree remains alive only in private gardens, propagated from samples collected in the 18th century.

————

Anti-environmentalists are quick to criticize the ESA for trampling private property rights. Yet when the Tennessee Valley Authority condemned ancestral Cherokee homeland and fifth-generation farms to make way for the lake behind Tellico Dam, the anti-environmentalists lined up on the dam-builders' side. The contest rumbled on, generating confusion as it went. More notoriety came to the ESA when the unfortunately named Furbish lousewort, a member of the snapdragon family declared endangered in 1978, became swept up into a battle over a proposed dam on the St. John River in Maine.

That same year, the Supreme Court upheld the lower court ruling in favor of the snail darter, noting that "the plain language of the Act, buttressed by its legislative history, shows clearly that Congress viewed the value of endangered species as incalculable." Congress responded by amending the ESA to establish a Cabinet-level committee empowered to permit the extinction of a species if salvaging it would cause undue social and economic hardship. This group, which included the chairman of the Council of Economic Advisors and the secretaries of agriculture and the army, among others, was dubbed "the God Squad."

The God Squad ruled unanimously that Tellico Dam should not be built. But in 1979 Congress pushed through a special measure to finish the project anyway, and the snail darter vanished from the site. Anticipating this outcome, biologists had begun transplanting the species to other stretches of the Tennessee River watershed. The relocations have met with mixed success. Some 2,500 snail darters swim in the nearby Hiwasee River today. Efforts to stock the Nolichucky River ended when recovery biologists found a related species already occupying the site—the sharphead darter.

Widespread searches netted other wild populations of snail darters after all, some as far away as Alabama, and in 1984, *Percina tanasi* was reclassified from endangered to threatened. But there are currently eight other kinds of darters listed as threatened and another six listed as endangered. The same river systems include various imperiled species of sturgeons, shiners, dace, and madtoms.

The Appalachians are among the oldest mountains on earth. Throughout their southern reaches, part of the vast Appalachian Plateau, species have been evolving and radiating into new niches for millions of years uninterrupted by the glaciers that scoured northern regions. As a result, the diversity seen in aquatic groups such as fish, crayfish, and mollusks of the American Southeast is as impressive as anything recorded in the tropics.

That whole faunas, not just scattered species, have become imperiled illustrates how thoroughly these river ecosystems have been altered by modern development within the space of a few decades. As we ask ourselves whether or not we are willing to save poorly known, unglamorous creatures like shiny pigtoes, they are, in effect, asking us how much more we are willing to degrade the waterways that are the life's blood of the region. Where darters and intact mussel beds persist, the chances are that it is safe to swim and eat the fish, that the river's bottom can be seen through a clear flow of water, and that the banks will be lush and green and a pleasure to walk along. Where the darters and mussel beds have disappeared, a visitor will more likely encounter sluggish water clouded with silt and contaminants, uninviting shores, and that pervasive modern sense of better days gone by.

The Tennessee watershed now has 54 dams. Number 55, proposed for the Duck River, was shelved not long ago, partly because of three endangered mussels. At the height of the snail darter controversy, few could even have imagined such a move. It doesn't happen very often, because the ESA is far more likely to modify development than to block it. Out of 98,237 endangered species consultations across the nation between 1987 and 1992, just 55 projects were stopped cold. Put another way, there have been relatively few impasses but a momentous number of conversations about how to work things out. It seems that we are on our way to embracing a truer definition of what good living conditions are—advancing in fits and starts perhaps, but advancing nonetheless.

NOWHERE TO HIDE

Extensive logging destroyed the vast tracts of forest needed to sustain the ivory-billed woodpecker, one of which posed for the above photo in 1938. The bird has most likely been extinct in the United States for decades, and though a population lingered in Cuba, there have been no recent sightings, and the species is now presumed extinct there.

3

Common Ground

THE MALLOW FAMILY, *MALVACEAE*, INCLUDES THE herb that is the original source of that sweet, puffy confection, the marsh mallow. It also includes the high mallow, whose leaves and flowers have been used medicinally, and a variety of showy cultivated species. The word "mauve" comes from the Old French name for mallow. Peter's Mountain mallow, *Iliamna corei*, with its rose-mauve petals, is one of 13 imperiled mallows in the U.S. The species was listed as endangered in 1986 after botanists searching the slopes of Peter's Mountain in Virginia managed to locate only four of the plants. In 1992, just when things looked darkest, a blaze swept through part of these woodlands, which had been protected from wildfire for decades. The next spring, a dozen mallow seedlings popped up through the scorched soil.

The welfare of a great many plants in both prairies and woodlands is tied to periodic fire, which stimulates germination, enriches the soil, and removes competitors. Peter's Mountain mallow may rely on fire more than most, botanists realized. It was they who had prescribed the blaze as an experiment. Another controlled burn the following year yielded 500 new mallow seedlings across the slopes. As soon as the Fish and Wildlife Service is reasonably certain that no other factors are holding the species back, the agency may remove the plant from the endangered list, declaring it recovered. That day should come in the very near future.

If most endangered species crises could be resolved even half as handily, controversies over the ESA would be little more than a footnote to these chapters. But for every case such as the mallow, there is one like that of the black-footed ferret, once found throughout the western Great Plains and laid low by widespread poisoning campaigns to eliminate "pests" such as prairie dogs and predators such as coyotes. Scientists have been struggling to recover the species since the mid-1960s, when only a single known population in South Dakota remained. Attempts at captive breeding failed, the wild group died out, and the biologists feared they had lost the species for good. Then in 1981 a group was discovered near Meeteetse, Wyoming. Better yet, this population appeared to be increasing. Suddenly, an epidemic of canine distemper reduced them to fewer than 20, and all the survivors were taken in for another try at captive breeding. Thus, as of the winter of 1986/87, the black-footed ferret finally did go extinct in the wild.

The last three wild California condors were also brought in during 1986 to save them from looming oblivion. As for the dusky seaside sparrow, an endangered subspecies once common along Florida's east coast, the last two left on earth were already in captivity. Both were male. One died in 1986. The other died the next year, alone in a cage, like the last passenger pigeon and Carolina parakeet. The survival of the black-footed ferret would depend on the fertility of eight adults nosing around the square-edged confines of the cages that held them.

"Their situation may be fragile," Don Kwiatkowski, a Wyoming veterinarian observed, "but I'm telling you, black-footed ferrets are about the hardiest animals I've ever worked on and the most stoic when they have a hurt. Even when they're suffering from a terminal illness, they hang on like nothing I've ever seen. You've got to admire them. This is one tough, tenacious creature we're trying to save here."

The captive ferrets succeeded in producing enough offspring for the recovery team to begin releasing some animals back into the sagebrush and shortgrass prairies of Wyoming's Shirley Basin by 1991. Despite being bolstered by more recruits from breeding facilities during each of the next several years, the new ferret colony never took hold. However, 40 additional ferrets were released into two other portions of their original range—Badlands National Monument in South Dakota and central Montana's Charles M. Russell National Wildlife Refuge—and they showed more encouraging rates of survival. Another 40 animals were added to each site in autumn of 1995.

As cold prairie winds blew the night sky clear of clouds, Lou Haneberry of the Fish and Wildlife Service recovery team lifted a panel to let a ferret out of the crate used to transport it to the Charles M. Russell refuge. Whether black-footed ferrets have a sense of wonder remains their secret. All Haneberry knew is that this animal had spent all its life cooped up, and now it was sliding those stretched-out forequarters down from the wooden box to sniff aromas wafting from the prairie dog burrow below and from hundreds of others that pocked the grassy valley between the dry hills. Glancing up, the animal's large, black eyes reflected the first stars it had ever seen without a screen in the way. Suddenly, the ferret was out and circling the burrow, nosing a sagebrush stem, then rippling over to sniff at the boots of a semicircle of biologists and volunteers gathered to watch. And then, flashing down into the labyrinth of the prairie dog's realm, it was gone. "Freedom," Haneberry whispered. That is what all the haggling, tinkering, and

BLACKFIN CISCO
Coregonus nigripinnis

————

Last seen 1960s

Like the Blue pike, the blackfin was a Great Lakes species that fell prey to overfishing and competition from introduced fish. It also suffered from parasitism by lampreys.

————

worrying finally comes down to, and it could not be any more right.

"It has to work," Haneberry said. "Our budget has been cut. We're running largely on volunteer labor and donations. And we may not have more ferrets to put out before long. Among the wild ferrets at Meeteetse, 99 percent of the breeding-age females would get pregnant. But the percentage has been dropping in the captive population. The average number of kits per litter has gone from 3.3 to more like 2. Half the kits are dying early. Sperm counts are low. Females are re-absorbing the fetuses. We've got animals with kinked tails, irregular teeth, extra toes, and cancer tumors."

These are all classic signs of inbreeding, not surprising in a species once pared down to eight breeding adults. Because some of those were related, the scientists think that all the ferrets in existence today come from three to, at most, five different genetic founders. Visible deformities such as kinked tails and odd toes typically herald the less visible but far more serious burdens of infertility, lowered immunity to disease, and an overall loss of vigor. Once enough deleterious genes concentrate in a small population, there may be no going back.

In the Everglades ecosystem, the last 30 to 50 Florida panthers in existence include individuals afflicted with kinked tails, fungal infections, hookworms, feline distemper, congenital heart defects, thyroid dysfunction, genital warts, the feline equivalent of AIDS, undescended testicles, and low sperm counts. To complicate matters, the big cats also suffer from serious contamination by mercury and pesticide residues.

Lower sperm counts, higher sperm irregularities, and smaller penis size have been recorded in Florida alligators, and similar reproductive abnormalities are showing up in other species, including humans across a broad geographic range. Though not all scientists consider the data conclusive, a common factor appears to be exposure to environmental contaminants, particularly chlorinated hydrocarbons, which mimic the potent hormone estrogen closely enough to disrupt normal metabolic pathways in vertebrates. With a record 1.25 billion pounds of herbicides, insecticides, and fungicides used in the U.S. during 1995, we clearly have more to consider than what ails the Florida panther. Larry Richardson, a biologist at Florida Panther National Wildlife Refuge, remarked, "Sometimes I think there's just one endangered species list, and all of us large mammals are on it. When one disappears, the rest of us move up a notch, that much closer to extinction."

Not far from Death Valley, Highway 95 passes through the old mining town of Beatty, Nevada. Here and in the surrounding Oasis Valley live the last few dozen Amargosa toads on the planet. An abrupt decline of amphibians has been noticed in many parts of both the U.S. and the world. Scientists remain puzzled as to the cause. Many suspect contaminants, since the amphibians' thin, moist skin makes them especially sensitive to harmful chemicals in the environment. The problem faced by the Amargosa toads, however, looks less complicated. Most of the desert springs and seeps vital to their existence have been hammered by thirsty livestock and feral burros, a non-native species that escaped from settlers and adapted to life in the drylands of the West. Karen Hoff, a herpetologist and environmental consultant from Las Vegas, has been trying to get the state and federal governments to list the toad as imperiled in order to begin protecting its habitat.

Hoff finally persuaded the Bureau of Land Management to fence off a few springs on public land used for grazing and mining. But the majority of the best spots for the toads are on private land; one is a spring-fed swimming pool in the backyard of a brothel. Officials have been reluctant to press for a listing of *Bufo nelsoni* for fear of stirring up another tempest in a region with a long-running Sagebrush Rebellion, an anti-government movement fueled chiefly by opposition to grazing regulations on federal land.

Hoff made her way to what had been a flourishing streambank along the edge of Beatty. "Last year, the town bulldozed it," she recalled. "They said it was for flood control. Basically, they wanted to keep a road to a trailer court open. Female toads can produce a huge number of eggs, and I'd found thousands of tadpoles here before. This year, I found 200."

Riparian, or streambank, zones are ribbons of biological diversity within the landscape. In addition to supporting aquatic life, they provide drinking water, lush vegetation for herbivores, and shelter, while the trees and brush lining the shores are essential to many nesting birds. Some 80 percent of all vertebrates in desert areas rely upon riparian areas at some stage of their lives. Yet more than 90 percent of these areas have been lost or seriously degraded in the Southwest.

The stream by Beatty had become a ditch encased by rock and gravel. Several Amargosa toads were swimming in it amid broken bottles and plastic litter, having no alternative but to cling to this short, precious stretch of water between the mouth of the spring above and the salty flats below, where the moisture evaporated into the desert air.

AS THE AMARGOSA TOAD'S SITUATION SUGGESTS, the endeavor to preserve vanishing wildlife often seems disturbingly haphazard. Creatures tend to be chosen for protection on the basis of what amounts to popularity contests influenced by media images and the organizational skills of special interest groups. Or, in the case of obscure species, because an academic happened to study a particular plant or animal in sufficient detail to perceive that it faced total eclipse. Or because, as ESA critics charge, somebody went out looking extra hard for rare flora or fauna to try and stave off an unwanted development.

Numbers of listed species and candidates have been mounting over the years. Budgets keep shrinking relative to the length of the list. And wildlife managers are left struggling with the terrible choice of which species to try to save. When all looks lost, the recovery specialists turn to captive breeding. As expensive as they are tricky, these programs are one reason nearly half the limited funds available for recovery have been channeled to a dozen or so species such as the California condor and black-footed ferret, and artificial propagation by itself does nothing to solve the problems that drove the species to its knees. For example, both prairie dogs and predators are still being poisoned by government agencies throughout most of the ferret's original range.

The ESA deserves credit for slowing the rate of extinction. Counting the ivory-billed woodpecker that lived in old-growth forests of the Southeast and was finally declared defunct in 1996, only eight out of the more than 900 listed species have met with oblivion so far. On the other hand, only a handful of species have completely recovered. Roughly one quarter of the listed species are now considered stable or improving—a respectable percentage, as biological systems take time to respond. Yet more than a third are still in decline, and the status of the rest is uncertain. Recovery plans have yet to be drawn for almost half the listed species, reflecting the lack of money appropriated for endangered species work. For some with plans, the recovery goal is a population lower than when the creature was first declared threatened or endangered.

In the meantime, an unknown number of species have vanished while waiting in line as candidates. Others in the twilight zone of existence are still alive only because of sheer serendipity. The weather happened to cooperate. A couple of key breeding females found mates. A land exchange secured essential habitat at the eleventh hour. Staging

ATLANTIC GRAY WHALE
Eschrichtius biggosus gibbosus

————

Last seen 1750

Though the Atlantic gray whale population was hunted to extinction by the mid-18th century, the Pacific gray whale population has recovered sufficiently to be taken off the Endangered Species list.

————

last-minute rescues one species at a time—sometimes referred to as ambulance-chasing or emergency ward conservation—may make for high drama and inspiring stories, but it is a risky way of safeguarding a biosphere. If our goal is to reverse the trend toward impoverishment of our living resources, we are falling short.

Biologists have started using another medical term: triage. In battlefield hospital stations, it means separating the incoming wounded into three groups: those that can hang on awhile, those that probably aren't going to make it even with help, and those that have a decent chance if you start operating. With regret, you put aside the first two groups and get to work on the third. Add the problem of how many small life-forms we can keep watch over in the first place, and the task of preserving biological diversity begins to feel overwhelming. How long can any society be expected to sustain an effort that generates so much uncertainty, acrimony, and guilt, not to mention extra work, before people start to either yield to despair or simply throw up their hands and walk away?

We don't have to continue frantically scrambling to save hundreds of different declining species, and we don't have to try and keep track of every minuscule creature out there. We have to save only one thing: the ecosystem to which they belong.

Conservation arose in the U.S. as a reaction to the reckless slaughter of charismatic animals, and attention has focused on the problem of excessive killing ever since. The public has been slow to recognize that the number one cause of vanishing wildlife in the U.S. today and around the world is vanishing habitat. There may be no obvious lethal force to be deflected, no heap of carcasses to trigger alarms. The changes are more often subtle and complex. A creature's range shrinks; food gradually becomes scarcer; reproduction tapers off; traveling farther to find food and mates, individuals become more vulnerable to predators and accidents. Before long, the species is sliding toward endangered status. Throw in human disturbance, disease, or a pollutant, and the species will qualify all the sooner. But if it had enough living space, it might be better able to cope with such pressures. The underlying problem remains habitat loss.

In today's world, an imperiled species is usually a symptom of an ecosystem out of balance. Several imperiled species in the same area amounts to a warning that at least part of the ecosystem is unraveling. There is seldom a quick and easy fix. But we do have the technology and the wealth to patch the broken parts, provided that we have the will. If we also take better care of the portions of the ecosystem that remain intact, the threatened and endangered list will become shorter.

In 1973 the ESA stated that, "The purposes of this Act are to provide a means whereby the ecosystems upon which endangered species and threatened species depend may be conserved...." Although the principle may seem clear, the shift from an emphasis on single species management to ecosystem management has been slow and difficult, for it requires seeing nature in a new way.

What is an ecosystem? It is an assemblage of organisms interacting with one another and their environment through a web of processes. It is the plants and animals you see in an area, but it is also the fungal networks and internal parasites that escape most people's notice, the rhythms of plant succession, the chemistry of the sediments, and the cycles of the weather. You can talk about an ecosystem on the scale of a tidepool or a single meadow. In general, however, an ecosystem is defined at the level of landscapes or watersheds and includes a variety of wildlife communities and habitats. It can be a region as large as, say, the Mojave Desert, which includes Las Vegas, Nevada.

Perhaps the least glitzy thing ever associated with that neon fantasyland is the desert tortoise, listed as threatened in 1989. In its slow, sure way, *Gopherus agassizii* is teaching us that conserving ecosystems means moving beyond the outmoded paradigm of people versus nature. It is a matter of managing people and nature together. There are ways to design plenty of room for both, but they call for a degree of planning and cooperation beyond what we're accustomed to.

Tortoises have been around 60 to 80 million years, from the days of the last dinosaurs through the era of Elvis Presley imitators. The genus *Gopherus* has inhabited this part of North America for between 5 and 12 million years. Desert tortoises first breed at about age 20 and may live a century, subsisting on a variety of desert grasses, herbs, and fruit. "An adult can go a year without eating or drinking, and females can store viable sperm from a mating for as long as four years," remarked University of Nevada-Reno tortoise researcher Ron Marlow, while hiking among creosote and saltbush in the pre-dawn glow of a summer's day, hoping to find tortoises out feeding before the sun drove them to cover.

By attaching threads to the animals so he could follow their travels, Marlow found that they "mine" for minerals to add to their diet, digging down to expose deposits among the rocks. The armored reptiles also excavate shallow pools to gather rainwater and scrape shallow daybeds, or pallets, in the shade of bushes. Their permanent home is a burrow one to three feet deep and as much as two yards long where they retire to aestivate when the vegetation becomes too dry to make it worth their while to keep foraging. Using a mirror to reflect sunlight into a burrow to see who might be at home, Marlow explained that the shady recesses are also habitat for kit foxes; jackrabbits; desert cottontails; burrowing owls; poorwills; Merriam's kangaroo rats; pocket mice; canyon mice; rattlesnakes; night and gopher snakes; western banded geckos; desert iguanas; and side-blotched, whiptail, desert spring, and zebra-tailed lizards; along with an array of invertebrates.

Once beyond the city's outskirts, you might find it hard to visualize any creature that dwells among the Mojave's stark contours as being threatened by human activity. This is the epitome of a lonely wasteland, in the opinion of many who pass through. Yet stockmen graze cattle across the desert. The herds compete with the tortoises for food, and exotic plants replace native vegetation in overgrazed and disturbed sites. Ranching, mining, and, increasingly, recreation have spread a grid of roads throughout the region. In California, the Mojave is crisscrossed by 14,000 miles of maintained asphalt or gravel roads and another 20,000 miles of dirt roads. All told, more than 90 percent of the western Mojave is now within a mile of a road. Then there are the ORVs (Off-Road Vehicles), which can go practically anywhere in between.

Every road removes habitat, and every off-road track crushes plants and compacts soil. Some popular desert playgrounds for ORVers have been churned into moonscapes. And every vehicle has the potential for squashing tortoises. "It's one of the major causes of death," Marlow said. "Some of the people driving around out here plink at tortoises, too; a fairly high percentage of carcasses found in the Mojave have bullet holes in them. Other people take tortoises home as pets."

Many just pause and pick up the reptiles for a closer look. Bad idea. When Marlow finally did locate a tortoise ambling by a Joshua tree, he made sure to tuck its tail down under the body before lifting the animal to inspect its condition. That way, the tortoise couldn't urinate on him, a common defense reaction. Not that was Marlow afraid of getting peed on. His concern was that it exhausts precious water the animal has stored—a supply that could prove critical to outlasting a drought.

Wherever people move out into the desert, they create garbage dumps that make scavenging a living from the desert a lot easier for the local ravens. And in addition, extra raven food comes in the form of animals crunched by vehicles; the birds regularly cruise above the road grids to search for dead or wounded lizards, jackrabbits—and tortoises.

AMISTAD GAMBUSIA
Gambusia amistadensis

————

Last seen 1977

A dam on the Rio Grande in Texas flooded the only spring in which this fish existed.

————

Transmission towers and telephone poles marching through the treeless countryside provide the birds with roosts and nesting sites where none existed before. As a result of our unintentional generosity, ravens have increased more than tenfold in some sections of the Mojave over the past quarter century, and they are preying heavily on juvenile tortoises, whose shells aren't hard enough to protect them against a powerful beak until they reach at least five years of age.

The tortoises had been on a downward trend for decades before an epidemic of mycoplasma, a respiratory disease, hit populations during the 1980s. They fell so sharply that the species was listed on an emergency basis. (Researchers estimate that there are anywhere from a few hundred thousand to a couple of million desert tortoises left. The fact that this species made the ESA list and the last few dozen Amargosa toads on earth have not is an example of the arbitrary species selection process.) Another cause of anxiety is the rapid sprawl of new housing and related activities. The Las Vegas Valley in the eastern Mojave was prime tortoise habitat. It is also one of the fastest growing metropolitan areas in the U.S., having more than doubled in size since 1980.

Ron Marlow was poking around the new 400,000-acre Desert Tortoise Reserve, consisting mainly of Bureau of Land Management property south of Las Vegas. It was set aside as part of a sweeping agreement called a Habitat Conservation Plan—HCP for short—between the Fish and Wildlife Service and Clark County, which takes in the city and some 7,000 square miles around it. Under an HCP, a project may be allowed to proceed within the habitat of a threatened or endangered species and may even "take" a limited number of animals. In return, whoever is responsible must come up with a plan to improve the species' overall chances of survival, usually through safeguarding and improving habitat elsewhere. Basically, an HCP is a kind of trade-off intended to make the ESA more flexible and encourage protection at the ecosystem level.

To offset the impacts of the expanding city, Clark County agreed to join in setting up the tortoise reserve and several Desert Wildlife Management Areas with tighter controls on grazing and ORV use. As part of the package, the county was buying up grazing permits from ranchers, compensating them in order to decrease the size of herds on prime tortoise habitat, and helping build a system of fences and underpasses for busy roadways to keep tortoises from getting squashed. The funding came from fees on new construction in the city and its burgeoning suburbs. Developers now pay the county $550 per acre plus $40 for every tortoise found and removed from property they intend to build upon.

Michelle Grasso, an ecologist hired by a large real estate corporation, literally walked in front of the bulldozers to get tortoises out of the way of new house sites. This was no perfunctory effort. Builders who failed to comply with HCP guidelines could be fined and have their development rights revoked. With raw land selling for between $40,000 and $100,000 per acre and houses for many times that amount, enormous profits were at stake. As the afternoon temperature climbed past 100 degrees, Grasso kept tramping past the survey flags, checking every scrape and hole in the ground for dome-backed reptiles.

The tortoises she drew out of their burrows were being relocated to a holding facility. She explained that in a unique exception to the ESA's rules, people able to prove that they could adequately care for and protect a tortoise within a properly fenced yard could adopt a displaced animal—a concession to the area's long tradition of keeping tortoises as pets and to the fact that nobody had yet figured out what else to do with the homeless tortoises. Among other biological uncertainties, worries over the spread of mycoplasma between groups had held up plans to put the tortoises out in the wild.

About 800 different types of plants, 41 fish, 9 amphibians, 54 reptiles, 392 birds, and 142 kinds of mammals live in Clark County. More than 50 of these are listed as threatened, endangered, or candidates, and more were being proposed for listing. The species that had become troublingly rare included blue diamond cholla cactuses, California bearclaw poppies, bi-colored beardstongues, chuckwalla lizards, gila monsters, razorback suckers, and southwestern otters.

To deal with so many imperiled life-forms individually would have been a dismaying challenge. But nearly all suddenly enjoyed better habitat protection because of the various Desert Wildlife Management Areas being set up within the same ecosystem through the tortoise HCP. The threatened desert tortoise played a similar role in spurring passage of the California Desert Protection Act in 1994. This bill fashioned 69 new wilderness areas, enlarged Joshua Tree and Death Valley National Monuments and awarded them national park status, and established 1.4-million-acre Mojave National Reserve. The beneficiaries include some of the same imperiled species found in Clark County, others more typical of California, and Mojave wildlife in general, from sidewinders to desert bighorn sheep. Fittingly, a desert tortoise rested on President Bill Clinton's desk and watched him sign the act.

Driving in the Las Vegas area, you pass billboards with a cartoon tortoise named Mojave Max urging citizens to respect, preserve, and enjoy the desert. He is the creation of the Clark County Public Information and Education Committee, organized as yet another part of the HCP. Representatives carry Max's message to thousands of schools in the area to teach children about desert ecology and conservation.

Of course, the animal symbolizes different things to different people. "The desert tortoise is to the Southwest what the spotted owl is to our friends the loggers in the Northwest," said Mark Trinko, of the Blue

Ribbon Coalition, which represents desert-users such as miners, stockmen, and ORV enthusiasts. Some 50 ORV races were being held each year in the desert terrain around Las Vegas, attracting tens of thousands of contestants and spectators. Under the HCP, the time and place were subject to tighter restrictions. Parts of courses were re-routed where tortoise burrows were found in the way. If a tortoise happened to be in the burrow, a monitor had to stand guard during the race.

"It's biologists just cooking up jobs for themselves," Trinko insisted. "The ESA is manipulated by Greenies. It's their weapon of choice against people. They want to lock everything up. We don't like the Desert Wildlife Management Area plans here in Clark County. We hardly have anyplace left to just go off-road cruising." Young and full of fiery indignation, Trinko looked ready for battle as he spread his group's information pamphlets onto a table. Then he added, "But we can live with the HCP because it leaves us enough room to do our races. We drove around with the Greenies agreeing on which roads to close and which to leave open. You won't see me and a Greenie arm-in-arm. Ever. But I think this HCP compromise is about as good as you'll find anywhere in the country."

Clark County's director of administrative services, Terry Murphy, was inclined to agree. "It's been a very public process," she observed from her perch high in a downtown office building. "We invited everyone in on the negotiations, and everyone stayed at the table. That includes ten government agencies, three state agencies, the county, and an assortment of private interests opposed to one another. It was the first time we had all talked together. We've accomplished something of great significance here: We cooperated, and there has been a heightened awareness of the desert environment in general. It certainly can't hurt to have these kinds of wild natural areas near what has become a fast-

SANTA BARBARA SONG SPARROW
Melospiza melodia

———

Last seen 1959

No sparrows have been observed since a 1959 fire destroyed their habitat on Santa Barbara island, California. In 1983 biologists gave up searching and declared the bird extinct.

———

growing urban center, and it can't hurt to keep all the different groups talking. That's what the HCP has done. If we hadn't carried it off, we would be where the Pacific Northwest is today with the spotted owl."

THAT BIRD AGAIN. No creature since the snail darter has put the spotlight on the ESA as fully as *Strix occidentalis caurina*, the threatened northern spotted owl of the Pacific Northwest's old-growth forests. After a government report suggested that almost eight million acres be put off-limits to chain saws, loggers hitched pants with empty pockets to suspenders saying, "Save a Logger, Eat an Owl," and families marched in the streets shouting that familiar refrain: "We're the ones endangered." A mere subspecies of bird, they said, was taking away thousands of jobs and millions of dollars in timber sales, making the entire region another victim of the conservation movement.

On the other side, some observed that if cutting was to continue at the pace seen through the 1980s, the woods workers would soon end up unemployed because most of the decent-size trees would be stumps. Americans donate significant sums of money to save the Amazonian rain forests, which have been reduced by about 30 percent. The Northwest's original temperate rain forests, among America's biologically richest ecosystems and owned mainly by the public, are nearly 90 percent sawed apart. More jobs have been lost to mechanization and the export of raw logs to Japan for processing than to regulations put in place to protect the woodland environment. From this standpoint, the owls and loggers alike are victims of a system that allowed timber corporations operating both on their own property and in national forests overseen by the Forest Service to choose short-term, clear-cut–and–run profits over sustainable harvests and thereby to reduce a magnificent green cathedral to stubble.

Shadow-laced, moss-softened, damp, and deep, those primeval

woodlands are also habitat for pine martens, pileated woodpeckers, and *Phenacomys*—voles that live in towering conifers. They are home as well to Pacific yew, eliminated as a "trash" shrub in clear-cuts until its bark yielded the cancer-fighting compound paclitaxel; for Roosevelt elk; for northern goshawks, declining along with their habitat; and for marbled murrelets, recently listed as threatened. The forest ecosystem also supports the habitats of seven migratory fish in the salmonid family: chinook, coho, chum, pink, and sockeye salmon, steelhead, and sea-run cutthroat trout.

Coho spend their first year or two in fresh water. Then, in preparation for life at sea, they grow massive amounts of new nerve tissue. This ability is unusual in vertebrates of such maturity, and investigators hold hope that it may lead to help for the 80,000 Americans who suffer disabling brain and spinal injuries every year. Salmon are also a health food. People who eat three ounces of salmon per week are half as likely to suffer cardiac arrest as people who eat none, studies suggest. The secret appears to be omega-3 oils. Believed to regulate the movement of electrolytes across cell membranes, they are unique to fish, especially active, cold water species such as salmon, herring, and mackerel.

Not that anyone who has eaten fresh salmon just for the taste or connected a fly line to the live voltage of steelhead needs to be convinced that such fish are worth saving. As late as 1992, commercial and sport fishing for salmonids added up to a billion-dollar-a-year industry, employing 60,000 people in the region, more than are employed by logging. Instead of jobs versus owls, the issue has become jobs versus jobs.

Amid a landscape originally blessed with an uncommon abundance of resources, timberman Gary Briggs, from Roseburg, Oregon, leaned out his pickup window and started right in on the President's Forest Plan, drawn up to resolve the old-growth controversy. "It lowers the annual timber cut from 4.5 billion board feet to 1.1 billion," he said. "Well, I used to cut 60 million myself each year with a crew of a hun-

dred. When the state said we couldn't cut within 25 feet of streams anymore, that was bad enough. Now the feds say to protect the owls and salmon we need a 300-foot setback from streams, even on company lands. I think that's a 'taking' of private property."

A logger came up to ask if Briggs had more work for him after this timber sale. Briggs could see the worry in the man's face, the bills coming due for the house, the truck. "How can I tell him I'm gonna go broke myself in six months, way things look," Briggs said when the man left. "This was a way of life for three generations in my family. I never even considered doing anything else. Now I wish to hell I had."

The "takings" issue of owls influencing where timber can be harvested on private lands later went all the way to the Supreme Court. The final judgment, which had implications for endangered species across the country, came down in favor of the spotted owl. But congressional representatives from the Northwest pushed through a measure that allows salvage logging operations to proceed unimpeded by the usual environmental regulations, claiming that these salvage operations are necessary to deal with the threat of fires and disease in forest stands. Noting that under the terms of the measure the harvest of green healthy timber is allowed within the same stands, opponents label the new salvage logging law a blatant attempt to circumvent the compromise crafted to protect spotted owls and the region's old-growth habitats.

On an autumn evening at an old cannery near Clifton, Oregon, Jack Marincovich, head of the Columbia River Fisherman's Protective Union, readied his boat for a night of fishing. He grew up netting salmon here in the lower river with his father, Andrew, who saw him off into the fading light.

As he let out several hundred feet of gill net, Marincovich shouted over the engine noise: "The thing I notice is that the water is a little lower, slower, and warmer each year." It was still lovely, though, reflecting a sky of moonlight behind rain clouds. Geese and gulls and a great horned owl called from the dark shores. When Jack hauled in after two hours, the net held one small chinook and three coho, or silvers. He made another set, brought it in around midnight. Empty. Marincovich turned for home. "These days our catch doesn't hardly pay gas for the boat," he grumbled. "It's sure not a livin' anymore. It's barely a pastime."

An ardent conservationist once said: "The salmon fisheries of the Columbia River are now but a fraction of what they were 25 years ago." That was president Theodore Roosevelt, arguing for fishing regulations in 1908. Few stopped to listen. On May 10, 1913, a single fishwheel—one of the great, paddlewheel-like contraptions that continually scooped fish from the river while revolving in the current—brought in 70,000 pounds of salmon. In 1991 the sockeye of the largest tributary, the Snake River, were listed as endangered after just four returned to spawn. The following year, the fall and spring-summer runs of Snake River chinook were declared threatened. In 1994 one lone Snake River sockeye returned to spawn.

Dams bear much of the blame. The sockeye have to negotiate eight big ones. And the overall equation includes such factors as overgrazing of riparian areas in Idaho's mountainous headwaters, which increases siltation of spawning beds, and our demand for French fries; each bite means more irrigation water sucked from the Snake to grow potatoes in Idaho's drylands. Nevertheless, generations of commercial fishermen kept right on overharvesting their resource, just as the loggers did.

Salmonids are also declining from California to northern Washington in rivers that have few or no dams. More than a hundred West Coast stocks (populations unique to a particular spawning stream)

GREAT AUK
Pinguinus imennis

————

Last seen 1844

Fishermen and explorers throughout the North Atlantic systematically slaughtered this flightless bird for its meat, oil, eggs, and feathers.

————

are extinct south of Canada, and more than 200 appear headed in that direction. The Pacific Rivers Council, an Oregon-based advocacy group, petitioned to list all Pacific coho stocks as endangered in the lower 48 states.

David Bayles, a council public lands specialist, headed up Canton Creek toward the mountainsides where newborn brooks learn to run and play. But he got there after a hard rain, and the young streams were muddied by runoff from steep, bare, bulldozed slopes. "We're in spotted owl country," he observed. "What's left of the big timber is mostly up here in the headwaters, and they contain most of the spawning areas." The sediments that smother salmon eggs and young come from clear-cuts and, even more, from the Northwest's quarter of a million miles of dirt logging roads. Both Oregon and Washington recently suspended commercial salmon fishing off their coasts. Environmentalists weren't responsible for the closures. Fisheries authorities trying to save the industry were; salmon counts were so low that the officials wanted as many as possible to pass safely by the fishing boats and run on upriver to breed.

Calls to save both owls and salmon went out early in the 1970s. The Forest Service and other agencies sidestepped them, promising greater sensitivity, new committees, more studies. In its 900-mile journey from the sea, a Snake River sockeye passes through more than 40 federal, state, local, and tribal jurisdictions. Indian fishermen were pointing fingers at sport fishermen, who blamed gillnetters, who blamed the offshore seiners, who blamed Canadian fishermen for taking Columbia-born salmon on their return from northern seas.

One of the latest solutions calls for increasing the survival of young salmon during their run to the ocean by drawing down dam reservoirs to help flush the fish along, much as the seasonal floods in untamed rivers do. This would leave less water later in the year for irrigators, barge operators, and hydropower producers, who oppose such a plan. Other suggestions include retrofitting dams with devices to help collect the fish so they can then be hauled by truck or barge around the whirling power turbines.

Salmon may be about to make the relatively cheap electricity long enjoyed by citizens and power-intensive industries such as aluminum smelters in the Northwest a thing of the past. But then you could argue that dams made cheap salmon a thing of the past first. At the upper-most end of the Columbia Basin, Montana is complaining that the reservoir drawdowns will ruin summer boating. Ironically, lowering lake levels for the sake of imperiled salmon downstream could have a negative effect on three Montana fish: the endangered pallid sturgeon; bull trout, a candidate for listing whose spawning stream habitats have been degraded by excessive logging in the Rockies; and rare westslope cutthroat trout, also hard-hit by logging.

Since the mid-nineties, the Forest Service has finally begun to reconsider the way it manages timberlands throughout the Columbia Basin ecosystem. The prospect is intimidating, as this watershed is roughly the size of France, but officials have come to recognize that if you're not operating on the same scale as nature is, your problems are only going to compound. Despite predictions of economic catastrophe, both Oregon and Washington have seen impressive net gains in jobs since the President's Forest Plan went into effect. Surveys show that people and new businesses are attracted to the region by its forests and rivers and the beauty of its landscapes—the quality of human life nourished by natural surroundings. In 1996 more than 150 timber corporations and logging contractors in the Northwest announced a voluntary initiative to avoid clear-cut logging in the future.

As with the desert tortoise, it took the ESA to force all the competing interests in the Northwest to get serious about fixing a common problem. It usually does. Typically, though, by the time the act is

triggered, a species at risk has slipped into critical condition, and more drastic measures may be required to revive it. Inevitably, the heavy hand leads many Americans to view the ESA as a symbol of intrusive big government, polarizing the issue so that a well-intended attempt to rescue a fellow creature gets swept up into ideological wars and endlessly delayed when time is of the essence for the species.

"We have some good resource laws on the books," said John Turner, former director of the Fish and Wildlife Service. "The National Environmental Policy Act, the Clean Water Act, the Federal Land Policy Management Act. But they haven't really been enforced. If they had been, we wouldn't see so many endangered species, especially on federal lands. The ESA takes all the heat because it has to do all the work."

THE CENTER FOR PLANT CONSERVATION SAYS that one in every five of the 20,000 plant species in the U.S. is in jeopardy and as many as 700 could be gone within a decade. The Nature Conservancy estimates that about 15 percent of all U.S. species are imperiled at the moment. Such figures explain why more than a few environmentalists have proposed replacing the Endangered Species Act with an Endangered Ecosystems Act. Whether or not that is politically practical remains to be seen, but it reinforces the importance of ecosystem management as a means of keeping a greater number of plants and animals from declining to a dangerously low point in the first place. If we don't start practicing preventive medicine as opposed to emergency ward care, how can we hope to ever get ahead in the race to conserve America's biological diversity?

Mike Scott, an ecologist at the University of Idaho Cooperative Research Unit, was asking such questions as he sat in front of a computer terminal and punched up a map of Idaho's vegetation. Over that he added maps showing the distribution of animal after animal, from lizards to big game. Using a powerful program called a geographic information system, Scott and his colleagues can superimpose hundreds of layers of such data to build a portrait of where biological diversity is most concentrated.

Comparing species-rich areas with the location of parks and preserves often reveals surprisingly little overlap, since, as grizzly bear recovery has made evident in the Rockies, many reserves were fashioned around scenery and recreation prospects rather than the habitat requirements of wildlife. "We call our technique gap analysis because it points out the gaps in our national network of protection," Scott said. "Planners can see how if they take care of, say, these two spots here, they will have 50 percent of the native diversity covered; add that spot, and the coverage rises to 70 percent, and so on. We don't need vast amounts of acreage to get to 90 percent protection. We just need to choose carefully."

An important perspective comes from studies of islands. You might expect two islands of different size in the same area to contain a similar array of species, with the smaller island simply having smaller populations of them. In reality, the smaller island will generally support far fewer species, especially among the bigger animals. Similarly, small, isolated patches of otherwise suitable habitat on the continent begin to lose species over time because of inbreeding and influences from surrounding areas. A number of species have disappeared from our national parks after those lands were fully protected.

The demise of each life-form can have a ripple effect, destabilizing the balance among survivors and triggering more extinctions. Throw in exotic invaders, and you have a situation like that of the Hawaiian Islands, where whole segments of the native flora and fauna are teetering on the brink. The story of wild habitats throughout the U.S. and the world in our era is one of continual fragmentation. They are becoming islands within a sea of human-inhabited, human-altered landscapes. We can declare them sanctuaries, but if they are too small, they simply can

CAROLINA PARAKEET
*Conuropsis carolinensis
carolinensis*

————

Last seen 1918

Farmers shot the parakeet as a nuisance bird and hunters killed them for their brilliantly colored plumage, which was used to decorate women's hats.

————

not do the job of sustaining biological diversity over time.

As a rule, an island one-tenth as large as another will carry only half as many species. The areas set aside for wildlife across the lower 48 states amount to significantly less than ten percent of the total land base. Does that mean we may expect to lose at least half our species in the years to come? If our reserves remain ecological islands, perhaps. But if they can be joined through well-chosen travel corridors, greenways, and the natural strands of waterways and riparian zones, then migration, dispersal, and genetic exchange may be able to keep the vital processes going within each unit indefinitely.

Thus a thousand-acre chunk is usually far more valuable to wildlife than ten hundred-acre fragments; two fragments linked by a corridor are more than twice as valuable than each one by itself. Connectivity. Multispecies planning. Long-range ecosystem management. Surrounded by satellite images and glowing screens, Mike Scott was a long way from paw prints on the forest floor. And yet in this digitized realm he was following tracks that lead back toward the ancient understanding of nature as an indivisible whole, a structure greater than the sum of its parts.

ECOLOGY IS NATURE'S VERSION OF ECONOMICS. Over the short term, what's good for the ecosystem may not always be the most profitable for a human economy. Over the long run, though, there is no difference between the two. Biological wealth translates into human wealth, and whatever doesn't make sense ecologically is going to leave future generations poorer.

According to Nathaniel Reed, former assistant secretary of the interior, "If ecosystem management is to succeed, it will only be with the willing assistance of private landholders." After all, the majority of habitat on which many threatened and endangered species exist is owned by corporations and individual citizens. They own nearly all of Orange County, where traffic sprays across southern California foothills remolded to fit beneath layers of new houses. In his Santa Ana office Tom Matthews, the county's director of planning, spread a highly detailed digital map on his table to show how remnants of California's coastal sage scrub community constitute only about 15 percent of the plant's former range. This analysis had been set in motion by the plight of the scrub's most celebrated resident, the California gnatcatcher, a twitchy-tailed little blue-gray bird that flits through brush low to the ground and mews like a kitten.

You can't not like a gnatcatcher. But as it became scarce, real estate developers were starting to call it the "southern spotted owl." Anxious to avoid another biopolitical train wreck, Secretary of the Interior Bruce Babbitt agreed to list the bird as threatened rather than endangered, which would allow the building industry an "incidental take" of the species if they participated in an HCP for coastal sage scrub, helping promote the gnatcatcher's recovery.

Whereas desert tortoises were still relatively abundant when the HCP for them was devised, the gnatcatchers were down to perhaps 2,500 breeding pairs. California already had a tough conservation planning process in place, though, and Orange County required builders to set aside 50 percent of new housing tracts as open space. The next step was to match those rules for growth to the gnatcatcher's. The selling point was that developers, like the birds, need certainty about the future. They can't afford to redesign projects every time another species in the area gets listed, and so much sage scrub had already been lost or fragmented that some 70 of the plants and animals dependent upon the habitat were in rocky shape along with the gnatcatcher. Make that 69; it looks as though Orcutt's spineflower just winked out once and for all while everybody was out focusing their binoculars on birds.

"Linking up the scattered islands of sage scrub has been the tough part," Matthews explained. "But we can plant native vegetation to build a habitat bridge. A whole cottage industry in habitat restoration is springing up in southern California." He tapped the map, calling it the kind of database that answers without rhetoric and emotion the questions people have been arguing over. Do we have enough open space? Do we have enough of the right kind in the right place? "Not only for gnatcatchers," he added, "but also for our riparian areas, our wetlands. And for the quality of life we want here. If we can pull this off in a region with 16 million people and land worth as much as a million bucks an acre, it ought to work for species protection and land-use planning anywhere in the country."

THE PRESCRIPTION FOR TURNING AROUND the long-standing pattern of American wildlife decline appears to be this: Fashion a web of well-chosen protected areas spanning the country. Our tools are old-fashioned natural history studies, new advances such as gap analysis, and a balanced combination of incentives to private landowners and direct government actions. The bigger the protected areas, the better, but they needn't be enormous. From the standpoint of safeguarding biodiversity, it is more important that those areas include representative samples from each of the country's ecosystems and as many of the biologically richest areas that have been identified as possible—and that they be linked.

A lot of the pieces are already in place: officially designated wilderness areas, state parks, and national parks and monuments. We have a less well known collection of natural areas to work with as well, one that contains more acreage than the national park system: the 92-million-acre national wildlife refuge system. It boasts at least one unit in every state, and over the last decade it has been adding more than seven new units a year.

In 1995, a federal refuge for native plants was set up along the sandy swells of Lake Wales Ridge in central Florida. The community that arose here, Florida oak scrub, contains one of the richest concentrations of unique flora in North America. The Lake Placid scrub mint yields a potent insect repellent. Scrub paw-paw produces a receptor for the neurotransmitter dopamine, which makes the plant of particular interest to medical researchers. The gopher apple is a choice food for gopher tortoises, an increasingly scarce relative of the desert tortoise. Gopher tortoise burrows, which may be 15 feet deep and 30 feet long, house 362 other species as varied as the rare indigenous Florida mouse; the threatened indigo snake, whose belly scales look like blue fire in the sun; gopher frogs; crickets; and spiders.

Almost half of the 550 kinds of vegetation present in this locale are found nowhere else on Earth. Forty-four of the plants are federally listed as threatened or endangered species or candidates, an additional 22 are on Florida's own state list, and the rest are all at risk, as are the Florida scrub jay, sand skink, and other fauna, because the habitat itself is in tatters. Over the past few decades, nine of every ten acres of Florida oak scrub were replaced by cleared pastures and furrowed citrus groves. With help from the Archbold Biological Station, the Nature Conservancy, and other conservation interests, the Fish and Wildlife Service has set about trying to acquire enough critical pieces of scrub and knit them together so that Lake Wales Ridge National Wildlife Refuge can sustain a functioning ecosystem. Almost every state in the Union has now signed on to the Gap Analysis Program, agreeing to map the distribution of native vegetation and animal populations to pinpoint the biologically richest areas within its borders. Florida has already taken the next step by creating a Conservation and Recreation Lands Program endowed with $300 million to acquire key habitats

FLORIDA RED WOLF
Canis rufus floridanus

———

Last seen 1925

The few wolves that managed to escape hunters eventually interbred with coyotes, which destroyed their genetic stock.

———

and establish corridors between them in the hope of ultimately linking wildlands throughout the state. The price is steep. But with 700 to 1,000 people moving in every week and throngs of tourists arriving through the winter, it is clear that whatever is not preserved is going to be developed very quickly. The choice is now or never. Since a great many of the people coming to Florida are attracted by its wildlife and by opportunities for outdoor recreation, planners view the money not as an expense but as a sound investment in the future. The program is well under way, and it is working.

We're getting there. The message is making its way to citizens and managers alike: Stop thinking in terms of single plants and animals. Stop thinking in terms of scattered, isolated reserves. Stop thinking in terms of us versus them. Think about connections. The natural processes are as important as the parts, and over the long run, you can't preserve one element without the others. Our efforts to apply the ESA have been teaching us as much, more clearly with each passing year. It may be the most important lesson we could learn on this green sphere, being one of the parts.

Above all, think of how to live together. We're not just saving species. We're engaged in a struggle to save the flux and flow and splendor of creation itself. It would be a mistake to enter a new millennium with anything less than the boldest of plans, or we may run low on living resources before the new era is barely underway. To allow the looming debacle of extinction to take place unopposed would be to fail every human who will inherit this world after us. We have other paths to choose from, and we must. There is no reason on earth to go into the future without all the good, wild company we can keep.

U.S. Endangered Species List

U. S. Endangered Species List

The pages that follow describe every plant and animal on the Endangered Species List as of July 1, 1996. Those whose status is given as **T** are threatened; those with an **E** are endangered. When a species appears more than once, each listing represents a distinct population. The populations with a status of **XN** are experimental colonies that have been reintroduced to the wild. A few species are listed as **S/A**, which means that while they are not endangered or threatened, they are too similar in appearance to species that are for the general public to tell the difference. Such is case with the American alligator, which is only on the list because it so closely resembles the endangered American crocodile.

The U.S. Fish and Wildlife Service has divided the country into seven administrative regions, above, and the list indicates the region inhabited by each species. Any species assigned to **region 9** is managed through the Service's main office in Washington, D.C. Those with a regional designation of **N** fall under the jurisdiction of the National Marine Fisheries Service.

VERTEBRATES

Mammals

3	E	Bat, gray (Myotis grisescens)
1	E	Bat, Hawaiian hoary (Lasiurus cinereus semotus)
3	E	Bat, Indiana (Myotis sodalis)
2	E	Bat, lesser (=Sanborn's) long-nosed (Leptonycteris curasoae yerbabuenae)
1	E	Bat, little Mariana fruit (Pteropus tokudae)
1	E	Bat, Mariana fruit (Pteropus mariannus mariannus)
2	E	Bat, Mexican long-nosed (Leptonycteris nivalis)
2	E	Bat, Ozark big-eared (Plecotus townsendii ingens)
5	E	Bat, Virginia big-eared (Plecotus townsendii virginianus)
9	T(S/A)	Bear, American black (Ursus americanus) [S/A]
6	T	Bear, grizzly (Ursus arctos)
4	T	Bear, Louisiana black (Ursus americanus luteolus)
1	E	Caribou, woodland (Rangifer tarandus caribou)
5	E	Cougar, eastern (Felis concolor couguar)
1	E	Deer, Columbian white-tailed (Odocoileus virginianus leucurus)
4	E	Deer, key (Odocoileus virginianus clavium)
6	E	Ferret, black-footed (Mustela nigripes)
6	XN	Ferret, black-footed (Mustela nigripes)
1	E	Fox, San Joaquin kit (Vulpes macrotis mutica)
2	E	Jaguarundi (Felis yagouaroundi cacomitli)
2	E	Jaguarundi (Felis yagouaroundi tolteca)
1	E	Kangaroo rat, Fresno (Dipodomys nitratoides exilis)
1	E	Kangaroo rat, giant (Dipodomys ingens)
1	E	Kangaroo rat, Morro Bay (Dipodomys heermanni morroensis)
1	E	Kangaroo rat, Stephens' (Dipodomys stephensi (incl. D. cascus)
1	E	Kangaroo rat, Tipton (Dipodomys nitratoides nitratoides)
9	T(S/A)	Lion, mountain (Felis concolor (all subsp. except coryi)) [S/A]
4	E	Manatee, West Indian (=Florida) (Trichechus manatus)
1	E	Mountain beaver, Point Arena (Aplodontia rufa nigra)
4	E	Mouse, Alabama beach (Peromyscus polionotus ammobates)
4	E	Mouse, Anastasia Island beach (Peromyscus polionotus phasma)
4	E	Mouse, Choctawahatchee beach (Peromyscus polionotus allophrys)
4	E	Mouse, Key Largo cotton (Peromyscus gossypinus allapaticola)
1	E	Mouse, Pacific pocket (Perognathus longimembris pacificus)
4	E	Mouse, Perdido Key beach (Peromyscus polionotus trissyllepsis)
1	E	Mouse, salt marsh harvest (Reithrodontomys raviventris)
4	T	Mouse, southeastern beach (Peromyscus polionotus niveiventris)
2	E	Ocelot (Felis pardalis)
1	T	Otter, southern sea (Enhydra lutris nereis)
1	XN	Otter, southern sea (Enhydra lutris nereis)
4	E	Panther, Florida (Felis concolor coryi)
6	T	Prairie dog, Utah (Cynomys parvidens)
2	E	Pronghorn, Sonoran (Antilocapra americana sonoriensis)
4	E	Rabbit, Lower Keys (Sylvilagus palustris hefneri)
4	E	Rice rat (=silver rice rat) (Oryzomys palustris natator)
N	T	Sea lion, Steller (=northern) (Eumetopias jubatus)
N	E	Seal, Caribbean monk (Monachus tropicalis)
N	T	Seal, guadalupe fur (Arctocephalus townsendi)
N	E	Seal, Hawaiian monk (Monachus schauinslandi)
5	T	Shrew, Dismal Swamp southeastern (Sorex longirostris fisheri)
4	E	Squirrel, Carolina northern flying (Glaucomys sabrinus coloratus)
5	E	Squirrel, Delmarva Peninsula fox (Sciurus niger cinereus)
5	XN	Squirrel, Delmarva Peninsula fox (Sciurus niger cinereus)
2	E	Squirrel, Mount Graham red (Tamiasciurus hudsonicus grahamensis)
5	E	Squirrel, Virginia northern flying (Glaucomys sabrinus fuscus)
1	E	Vole, Amargosa (Microtus californicus scirpensis)
4	E	Vole, Florida salt marsh (Microtus pennsylvanicus dukecampbelli)
2	E	Vole, Hualapai Mexican (Microtus mexicanus hualpaiensis)
N	E	Whale, blue (Balaenoptera musculus)
N	E	Whale, bowhead (Balaena mysticetus)
N	E	Whale, finback (Balaenoptera physalus)
N	E	Whale, humpback (Megaptera novaeangliae)
N	E	Whale, right (Balaena glacialis (incl. australis))
N	E	Whale, Sei (Balaenoptera borealis)
N	E	Whale, sperm (Physeter macrocephalus (=catodon))
3	E	Wolf, gray (Canis lupus)
3	T	Wolf, gray (Canis lupus)
6	XN	Wolf, gray (Canis lupus)
4	E	Wolf, red (Canis rufus)
4	XN	Wolf, red (Canis rufus)
4	E	Woodrat, Key Largo (Neotoma floridana smalli)

Birds

1	E	`Akepa, Hawaii (honeycreeper) (Loxops coccineus coccineus)
1	E	`Akepa, Maui (honeycreeper) (Loxops coccineus ochraceus)
1	E	`Akialoa, Kauai (honeycreeper) (Hemignathus procerus)
1	E	`Akiapola`au (honeycreeper) (Hemignathus munroi)
4	E	Blackbird, yellow-shouldered (Agelaius xanthomus)
2	E	Bobwhite, masked (quail) (Colinus virginianus ridgwayi)
1	E	Broadbill, Guam (Myiagra freycineti)
4	T	Caracara, Audubon's crested (Polyborus plancus audubonii)
1	E	Condor, California (Gymnogyps californianus)
1	E	Coot, Hawaiian (=`alae-ke`oke`o) (Fulica americana alai)
4	E	Crane, Mississippi sandhill (Grus canadensis pulla)
2	E	Crane, whooping (Grus americana)
4	XN	Crane, whooping (Grus americana)
1	E	Creeper, Hawaii (Oreomystis mana)
1	E	Creeper, Molokai (=kakawahie) (Paroreomyza flammea)
1	E	Creeper, Oahu (=alauwahio) (Paroreomyza maculata)
1	E	Crow, Hawaiian (=`alala) (Corvus hawaiiensis)

region / status / species

region	status	species
1	E	Crow, Mariana (Corvus kubaryi)
7	E	Curlew, Eskimo (Numenius borealis)
1	E	Duck, Hawaiian (=koloa) (Anas wyvilliana)
1	E	Duck, Laysan (Anas laysanensis)
3	T	Eagle, bald (Haliaeetus leucocephalus)
7	T	Eider, spectacled (Somateria fischeri)
1	E	Falcon, American peregrine (Falco peregrinus anatum)
2	E	Falcon, northern aplomado (Falco femoralis septentrionalis)
9	E(S/A)	Falcon, peregrine (Falco peregrinus) [S/A]
1	E	Finch, Laysan (honeycreeper) (Telespyza cantans)
1	E	Finch, Nihoa (honeycreeper) (Telespyza ultima)
2	E	Flycatcher, Southwestern willow (Empidonax traillii extimus)
1	T	Gnatcatcher, coastal California (Polioptila californica californica)
7	T	Goose, Aleutian Canada (Branta canadensis leucopareia)
1	E	Goose, Hawaiian (=nene) (Nesochen sandvicensis)
1	E	Hawk, Hawaiian (=io) (Buteo solitarius)
4	E	Hawk, Puerto Rican broad-winged (Buteo platypterus brunnescens)
4	E	Hawk, Puerto Rican sharp-shinned (Accipiter striatus venator)
1	E	Honeycreeper, crested (=`akohekohe) (Palmeria dolei)
4	T	Jay, Florida scrub (Aphelocoma coerulescens coerulescens)
1	E	Kingfisher, Guam Micronesia (Halcyon cinnamomina cinnamomina)
4	E	Kite, Everglade snail (Rostrhamus sociabilis plumbeus)
1	E	Mallard, Mariana (Anas oustaleti)
1	E	Megapode, Micronesian (=La Perouse's) (Megapodius laperouse)
1	E	Millerbird, Nihoa (old world warbler) (Acrocephalus familiaris kingi)
1	T	Monarch, Tinian (Monarcha takatsukasae)
1	E	Moorhen (=gallinule), Hawaiian common (Gallinula chloropus sandvicensis)
1	E	Moorhen (=gallinule), Mariana common (Gallinula chloropus guami)
1	T	Murrelet, marbled (Brachyramphus marmoratus marmoratus)
4	E	Nightjar, Puerto Rican (=whip-poor-will) (Caprimulgus noctitherus)
1	E	Nukupu`u (honeycreeper) (Hemignathus lucidus)
1	E	`O`o, Kauai (=`o`o `a`a) (honeyeater) (Moho braccatus)
1	E	`O`u (honeycreeper) (Psittirostra psittacea)
2	T	Owl, Mexican spotted (Strix occidentalis lucida)
1	T	Owl, northern spotted (Strix occidentalis caurina)
1	E	Palila (honeycreeper) (Loxioides bailleui)
4	E	Parrot, Puerto Rican (Amazona vittata)
1	E	Parrotbill, Maui (honeycreeper) (Pseudonestor xanthophrys)
1	E	Pelican, brown (Pelecanus occidentalis)
1	E	Petrel, Hawaiian dark-rumped (Pterodroma phaeopygia sandwichensis)
4	E	Pigeon, Puerto Rican plain (Columba inornata wetmorei)
3	E	Plover, piping (Charadrius melodus)
3	T	Plover, piping (Charadrius melodus)
1	T	Plover, western snowy (Charadrius alexandrinus nivosus)
1	E	Po`ouli (honeycreeper) (Melamprosops phaeosoma)
2	E	Prairie-chicken, Attwater's greater (Tympanuchus cupido attwateri)
1	E	Rail, California clapper (Rallus longirostris obsoletus)
1	E	Rail, Guam (Rallus owstoni)
1	XN	Rail, Guam (Rallus owstoni)
1	E	Rail, light-footed clapper (Rallus longirostris levipes)
2	E	Rail, Yuma clapper (Rallus longirostris yumanensis)
1	T	Shearwater, Newell's Townsend's (formerly Manx) (=`a`o) (Puffinus auricularis newelli)
1	E	Shrike, San Clemente loggerhead (Lanius ludovicianus mearnsi)
4	E	Sparrow, Cape Sable seaside (Ammodramus maritimus mirabilis)
4	E	Sparrow, Florida grasshopper (Ammodramus savannarum floridanus)
1	T	Sparrow, San Clemente sage (Amphispiza belli clementeae)
1	E	Stilt, Hawaiian (=ae`o) (Himantopus mexicanus knudseni)
4	E	Stork, wood (Mycteria americana)
1	E	Swiftlet, Mariana gray (=vanikoro) (Aerodramus vanikorensis bartschi)
1	E	Tern, California least (Sterna antillarum browni)
3	E	Tern, least (Sterna antillarum)
5	E	Tern, roseate (Sterna dougallii dougallii)
5	T	Tern, roseate (Sterna dougallii dougallii)
1	E	Thrush, large Kauai (Myadestes myadestinus)
1	E	Thrush, Molokai (=oloma`o) (Myadestes lanaiensis rutha)
1	E	Thrush, small Kauai (=puaiohi) (Myadestes palmeri)
2	T	Towhee, Inyo California (=brown) (Pipilo crissalis eremophilus)
2	E	Vireo, black-capped (Vireo atricapillus)
1	E	Vireo, least Bell's (Vireo bellii pusillus)
1	E	Warbler, nightingale reed (Acrocephalus luscinia)
4	E	Warbler, Bachman's (Vermivora bachmanii)
2	E	Warbler, golden-cheeked (Dendroica chrysoparia)
3	E	Warbler, Kirtland's (Dendroica kirtlandii)
1	E	White-eye, bridled (Zosterops conspicillatus conspicillatus)
4	E	Woodpecker, ivory-billed (Campephilus principalis)
4	E	Woodpecker, red-cockaded (Picoides borealis)

Reptiles

region	status	species
9	T(S/A)	Alligator, American (Alligator mississippiensis) [S/A]
4	E	Anole, Culebra Island giant (Anolis roosevelti)
4	T	Boa, Mona (Epicrates monensis monensis)
4	E	Boa, Puerto Rican (Epicrates inornatus)
4	E	Boa, Virgin Islands tree (Epicrates monensis granti)
4	E	Crocodile, American (Crocodylus acutus)
4	E	Gecko, Monito (Sphaerodactylus micropithecus)
4	T	Iguana, Mona ground (Cyclura stejnegeri)
1	E	Lizard, blunt-nosed leopard (Gambelia silus)
1	T	Lizard, Coachella Valley fringe-toed (Uma inornata)
1	T	Lizard, Island night (Xantusia riversiana)
4	E	Lizard, St. Croix ground (Ameiva polops)
2	T	Rattlesnake, New Mexican ridge-nosed (Crotalus willardi obscurus)
4	T	Skink, bluetail (=blue-tailed) mole (Eumeces egregius lividus)
4	T	Skink, sand (Neoseps reynoldsi)
4	T	Snake, Atlantic salt marsh (Nerodia clarkii taeniata)
2	T	Snake, Concho water (Nerodia paucimaculata)
4	T	Snake, eastern indigo (Drymarchon corais couperi)
1	T	Snake, giant garter (Thamnophis gigas)
1	E	Snake, San Francisco garter (Thamnophis sirtalis tetrataenia)
1	T	Tortoise, desert (Gopherus agassizii)
9	T(S/A)	Tortoise, desert (Gopherus (=Xerobates, =Scaptochelys) agassizii)
4	T	Tortoise, gopher (Gopherus polyphemus)
4	E	Turtle, Alabama redbelly (=red-bellied) (Pseudemys alabamensis)
4	T	Turtle, flattened musk (Sternotherus depressus)
2	T	Turtle, green sea (Chelonia mydas)
2	E	Turtle, green sea (Chelonia mydas)
2	E	Turtle, hawksbill sea (Eretmochelys imbricata)
2	E	Turtle, Kemp's (=Atlantic) ridley sea (Lepidochelys kempii)
2	E	Turtle, leatherback sea (Dermochelys coriacea)
2	T	Turtle, loggerhead sea (Caretta caretta)
2	T	Turtle, olive (=Pacific) ridley sea (Lepidochelys olivacea)
5	E	Turtle, Plymouth redbelly (=red-bellied) (Pseudemys rubriventris bangsi)
4	T	Turtle, ringed map (=sawback) (Graptemys oculifera)
4	T	Turtle, yellow-blotched map (=sawback) (Graptemys flavimaculata)

Amphibians

region	status	species
4	T	Coqui, golden (Eleutherodactylus jasperi)
1	T	Frog, California red-legged (Rana aurora draytoni)
5	T	Salamander, Cheat Mountain (Plethodon nettingi)
1	E	Salamander, desert slender (Batrachoseps aridus)
4	E	Salamander, Red Hills (Phaeognathus hubrichti)
2	T	Salamander, San Marcos (Eurycea nana)
1	E	Salamander, Santa Cruz long-toed (Ambystoma macrodactylum croceum)
5	E	Salamander, Shenandoah (Plethodon shenandoah)
2	E	Salamander, Texas blind (Typhlomolge rathbuni)
1	E	Toad, arroyo southwestern (Bufo microscaphus californicus)
2	E	Toad, Houston (Bufo houstonensis)
4	T	Toad, Puerto Rican crested (Peltophryne lemur)
6	E	Toad, Wyoming (Bufo hemiophrys baxteri)

Fishes

region	status	species
2	T	Catfish, Yaqui (Ictalurus pricei)
4	E	Cavefish, Alabama (Speoplatyrhinus poulsoni)
4	T	Cavefish, Ozark (Amblyopsis rosae)
6	E	Chub, bonytail (Gila elegans)
1	E	Chub, Borax Lake (Gila boraxobius)
2	T	Chub, Chihuahua (Gila nigrescens)
6	E	Chub, humpback (Gila cypha)
1	T	Chub, Hutton tui (Gila bicolor ssp.)
1	E	Chub, Mohave tui (Gila bicolor mohavensis)
1	E	Chub, Oregon (Oregonichthys (=Hybopsis) crameri)
1	E	Chub, Owens tui (Gila bicolor snyderi)
1	E	Chub, Pahranagat roundtail (=bonytail) (Gila robusta jordani)
4	T	Chub, slender (Erimystax (=Hybopsis) cahni)
2	T	Chub, Sonora (Gila ditaenia)
4	T	Chub, spotfin (=turquoise shiner) (Cyprinella (=Hybopsis) monacha)

147

6	E	Chub, Virgin River (Gila robusta semidnuda)
2	E	Chub, Yaqui (Gila purpurea)
1	E	Cui-ui (Chasmistes cujus)
1	E	Dace, Ash Meadows speckled (Rhinichthys osculus nevadensis)
4	T	Dace, blackside (Phoxinus cumberlandensis)
1	E	Dace, Clover Valley speckled (Rhinichthys osculus oligoporus)
1	T	Dace, desert (Eremichthys acros)
1	T	Dace, Foskett speckled (Rhinichthys osculus ssp.)
1	E	Dace, Independence Valley speckled (Rhinichthys osculus lethoporus)
6	E	Dace, Kendall Warm Springs (Rhinichthys osculus thermalis)
1	E	Dace, Moapa (Moapa coriacea)
4	E	Darter, amber (Percina antesella)
4	T	Darter, bayou (Etheostoma rubrum)
4	E	Darter, bluemask (=jewel) (Etheostoma (Doration) sp.)
4	E	Darter, boulder (=Elk River) (Etheostoma wapiti)
4	T	Darter, Cherokee (Etheostoma (Ulocentra) sp.)
4	E	Darter, duskytail (Etheostoma (Catonotus) sp.)
4	E	Darter, Etowah (Etheostoma etowahae)
2	E	Darter, fountain (Etheostoma fonticola)
4	T	Darter, goldline (Percina aurolineata)
2	T	Darter, leopard (Percina pantherina)
5	E	Darter, Maryland (Etheostoma sellare)
3	T	Darter, Niangua (Etheostoma nianguae)
4	E	Darter, Okaloosa (Etheostoma okaloosae)
4	T	Darter, relict (Etheostoma (Catonotus) chienense)
4	T	Darter, slackwater (Etheostoma boschungi)
4	T	Darter, snail (Percina tanasi)
4	E	Darter, watercress (Etheostoma nuchale)
2	E	Gambusia, Big Bend (Gambusia gaigei)
2	E	Gambusia, Clear Creek (Gambusia heterochir)
2	E	Gambusia, Pecos (Gambusia nobilis)
2	E	Gambusia, San Marcos (Gambusia georgei)
1	E	Goby, tidewater (Eucyclogobius newberryi)
4	E	Logperch, Conasauga (Percina jenkinsi)
5	E	Logperch, Roanoke (Percina rex)
6	T	Madtom, Neosho (Noturus placidus)
4	E	Madtom, pygmy (Noturus stanauli)
3	E	Madtom, Scioto (Noturus trautmani)
4	E	Madtom, Smoky (Noturus baileyi)
4	T	Madtom, yellowfin (Noturus flavipinnis)
4	XN	Madtom, yellowfin (Noturus flavipinnis)
2	T	Minnow, loach (Rhinichthys (=Tiaroga) cobitis)
2	E	Minnow, Rio Grande silvery (Hybognathus amarus)
1	E	Poolfish (=killifish), Pahrump (Empetrichthys latos)
1	E	Pupfish, Ash Meadows Amargosa (Cyprinodon nevadensis mionectes)
2	E	Pupfish, Comanche Springs (Cyprinodon elegans)
2	E	Pupfish, desert (Cyprinodon macularius)
1	E	Pupfish, Devils Hole (Cyprinodon diabolis)
2	E	Pupfish, Leon Springs (Cyprinodon bovinus)
1	E	Pupfish, Owens (Cyprinodon radiosus)
1	E	Pupfish, Warm Springs (Cyprinodon nevadensis pectoralis)
N	T	Salmon, chinook (winter Sacramento R.) (Oncorhynchus tshawytscha)
N	T	Salmon, chinook (spring/summer Snake R.) (Oncorhynchus tshawytscha)
N	T	Salmon, chinook (fall Snake R.) (Oncorhynchus tshawytscha)
N	E	Salmon, sockeye (=red, =blueback) (Oncorhynchus nerka)
4	T	Sculpin, pygmy (Cottus pygmaeus)
2	T	Shiner, beautiful (Cyprinella (=Notropis) formosa)
4	T	Shiner, blue (Cyprinella (=Notropis) caerulea)
4	E	Shiner, Cahaba (Notropis cahabae)
4	E	Shiner, Cape Fear (Notropis mekistocholas)
4	E	Shiner, Palezone (Notropis sp.)
2	T	Shiner, Pecos bluntnose (Notropis simus pecosensis)
4	T	Silverside, Waccamaw (Menidia extensa)
1	T	Smelt, delta (Hypomesus transpacificus)
2	T	Spikedace (Meda fulgida)
1	T	Spinedace, Big Spring (Lepidomeda mollispinis pratensis)
2	T	Spinedace, Little Colorado (Lepidomeda vittata)
1	E	Spinedace, White River (Lepidomeda albivallis)
1	E	Springfish, Hiko White River (Crenichthys baileyi grandis)
1	T	Springfish, Railroad Valley (Crenichthys nevadae)
1	E	Springfish, White River (Crenichthys baileyi baileyi)
6	E	Squawfish, Colorado (Ptychocheilus lucius)
6	XN	Squawfish, Colorado (Ptychocheilus lucius)
1	E	Stickleback, unarmored threespine (Gasterosteus aculeatus williamsoni)
4	T	Sturgeon, Gulf (Acipenser oxyrhynchus desotoi)
6	E	Sturgeon, pallid (Scaphirhynchus albus)
N	E	Sturgeon, shortnose (Acipenser brevirostrum)
1	E	Sturgeon, white (Kootenai River pop.) (Acipenser transmontanus)
6	E	Sucker, June (Chasmistes liorus)
1	E	Sucker, Lost River (Deltistes luxatus)
1	E	Sucker, Modoc (Catostomus microps)
6	E	Sucker, razorback (Xyrauchen texanus)
1	E	Sucker, shortnose (Chasmistes brevirostris)
1	T	Sucker, Warner (Catostomus warnerensis)
2	E	Topminnow, Gila (incl. Yaqui) (Poeciliopsis occidentalis)
2	T	Trout, Apache (=Arizona) (Oncorhynchus (=Salmo) apache)
2	E	Trout, Gila (Oncorhynchus (=Salmo) gilae)
6	T	Trout, greenback cutthroat (Oncorhynchus (=Salmo) clarki stomias)
1	T	Trout, Lahontan cutthroat (Oncorhynchus (=Salmo) clarki henshawi)
1	T	Trout, Little Kern golden (Oncorhynchus (=Salmo) aguabonita whitei)
1	T	Trout, Paiute cutthroat (Oncorhynchus (=Salmo) clarki seleniris)
6	E	Woundfin (Plagopterus argentissimus)
6	XN	Woundfin (Plagopterus argentissimus)

INVERTEBRATES

Clams

4	E	Acornshell, southern (Epioblasma othcaloogensis)
4	E	Clubshell, black (=Curtus' mussel) (Pleurobema curtum)
4	E	Clubshell, ovate (Pleurobema perovatum)
4	E	Clubshell, southern (Pleurobema decisum)
5	E	Clubshell (Pleurobema clava)
4	E	Combshell, southern (=penitent mussel) (Epioblasma penita)
4	E	Combshell, upland (Epioblasma metastriata)
4	E	Elktoe, Appalachian (Alasmidonta raveneliana)
4	E	Fanshell (Cyprogenia stegaria)
4	T	Fatmucket, Arkansas (Lampsilis powelli)
4	E	Heelsplitter, Carolina (Lasmigona decorata)
4	T	Heelsplitter, inflated (Potamilus inflatus)
4	E	Kidneyshell, triangular (Ptychobranchus greeni)
4	E	Lampmussel, Alabama (Lampsilis virescens)
4	T	Moccasinshell, Alabama (Medionidus acutissimus)
4	E	Moccasinshell, Coosa (Medionidus parvulus)
4	T	Mucket, orange-nacre (Lampsilis perovalis)
5	E	Mussel, dwarf wedge (Alasmidonta heterodon)
4	E	Mussel, ring pink (=golf stick pearly) (Obovaria retusa)
3	E	Mussel, winged mapleleaf (Quadrula fragosa)
4	T	Pearlshell, Louisiana (Margaritifera hembeli)
4	E	Pearlymussel, Appalachian monkeyface (Quadrula sparsa)
4	E	Pearlymussel, birdwing (Conradilla caelata)
4	E	Pearlymussel, cracking (Hemistena lata)
4	E	Pearlymussel, Cumberland bean (Villosa trabalis)
4	E	Pearlymussel, Cumberland monkeyface (Quadrula intermedia)
3	E	Pearlymussel, Curtis' (Epioblasma (=Dysnomia) florentina curtisi)
4	E	Pearlymussel, dromedary (Dromus dromas)
4	E	Pearlymussel, green-blossom (Epioblasma torulosa gubernaculum)
3	E	Pearlymussel, Higgins' eye (Lampsilis higginsi)
4	E	Pearlymussel, little-wing (Pegias fabula)
4	E	Pearlymussel, orange-foot pimple back (Plethobasus cooperianus)
4	E	Pearlymussel, pale lilliput (Toxolasma cylindrellus)
4	E	Pearlymussel, pink mucket (Lampsilis abrupta)
4	E	Pearlymussel, purple cat's paw (Epioblasma obliquata obliquata)
4	E	Pearlymussel, tubercled-blossom (Epioblasma torulosa torulosa)
4	E	Pearlymussel, turgid-blossom (Epioblasma turgidula)
3	E	Pearlymussel, white cat's paw (Epioblasma obliquata perobliqua (=sulcata delicata))
4	E	Pearlymussel, white wartyback (Plethobasus cicatricosus)
4	E	Pearlymussel, yellow-blossom (Epioblasma florentina florentina)
4	E	Pigtoe, Cumberland (=Cumberland pigtoe mussel) (Pleurobema gibberum)
4	E	Pigtoe, dark (Pleurobema furvum)
4	E	Pigtoe, fine-rayed (Fusconaia cuneolus)
4	E	Pigtoe, flat (=Marshall's mussel) (Pleurobema marshalli)
4	E	Pigtoe, heavy (=Judge Tait's mussel) (Pleurobema taitianum)

Region	Status	Species
4	E	Pigtoe, rough (Pleurobema plenum)
4	E	Pigtoe, shiny (Fusconaia cor (=edgariana))
4	E	Pigtoe, southern (Pleurobema georgianum)
4	E	Pocketbook, fat (Potamilus (=Proptera) capax)
4	T	Pocketbook, fine-lined (Lampsilis altilis)
4	E·	Pocketbook, speckled (Lampsilis streckeri)
5	E	Riffleshell, northern (Epioblasma torulosa rangiana)
4	E	Riffleshell, tan (Epioblasma walkeri)
2	E	Rock-pocketbook, Ouachita (=Wheeler's pearly mussel) (Arkansia wheeleri)
5	E	Spinymussel, James River (=Virginia) (Pleurobema collina)
4	E	Spinymussel, Tar River (Elliptio steinstansana)
4	E	Stirrupshell (Quadrula stapes)

Snails

Region	Status	Species
6	E	Ambersnail, Kanab (Oxyloma haydeni kanabensis)
1	E	Limpet, Banbury Springs (Lanx sp.)
4	E	Marstonia (snail), royalobese) (Pyrgulopsis (=Marstonia) ogmoraphe)
4	E	Riversnail, Anthony's (Athearnia anthonyi)
4	T	Shagreen, Magazine Mountain (Mesodon magazinensis)
1	T	Snail, Bliss Rapids (Taylorconcha serpenticola)
5	T	Snail, Chittenango ovate amber (Succinea chittenangoensis)
5	T	Snail, flat-spired three-toothed (Triodopsis platysayoides)
3	E	Snail, Iowa Pleistocene (Discus macclintocki)
1	E	Snail, Morro shoulderband (=banded dune) (Helminthoglypta walkeriana)
4	T	Snail, noonday (Mesodon clarki nantahala)
4	T	Snail, painted snake coiled forest (Anguispira picta)
1	E	Snail, Snake River physa (Physa natricina)
4	T	Snail, Stock Island tree (Orthalicus reses (not incl. nesodryas))
4	E	Snail, tulotoma (=Alabama live-bearing) (Tulotoma magnifica)
1	E	Snail, Utah valvata (Valvata utahensis)
5	E	Snail, Virginia fringed mountain (Polygyriscus virginianus)
1	E	Snails, Oahu tree (Achatinella spp.)
2	E	Springsnail, Alamosa (Tryonia alamosae)
1	E	Springsnail, Bruneau Hot (Pyrgulopsis bruneauensis)
1	E	Springsnail, Idaho (Fontelicella idahoensis)
2	E	Springsnail, Socorro (Pyrgulopsis neomexicana)

Insects

Region	Status	Species
5	E	Beetle, American burying (=giant carrion) (Nicrophorus americanus)
2	E	Beetle, Coffin Cave mold (Batrisodes texanus)
1	T	Beetle, delta green ground (Elaphrus viridis)
3	E	Beetle, Hungerford's crawling water (Brychius hungerfordi)
2	E	Beetle, Kretschmarr Cave mold (Texamaurops reddelli)
5	T	Beetle, northeastern beach tiger (Cicindela dorsalis dorsalis)
5	T	Beetle, Puritan tiger (Cicindela puritana)
2	E	Beetle, Tooth Cave ground (Rhadine persephone)
1	T	Beetle, valley elderberry longhorn (Desmocerus californicus dimorphus)
1	T	Butterfly, bay checkerspot (Euphydryas editha bayensis)
1	E	Butterfly, El Segundo blue (Euphilotes battoides allyni)
5	E	Butterfly, Karner blue (Lycaeides melissa samuelis)
1	E	Butterfly, Lange's metalmark (Apodemia mormo langei)
1	E	Butterfly, lotis blue (Lycaeides argyrognomon lotis)
1	E	Butterfly, mission blue (Icaricia icarioides missionensis)
3	E	Butterfly, Mitchell's satyr (Neonympha mitchellii mitchellii)
1	E	Butterfly, Myrtle's silverspot (Speyeria zerene myrtleae)
1	T	Butterfly, Oregon silverspot (Speyeria zerene hippolyta)
1	E	Butterfly, Palos Verdes blue (Glaucopsyche lygdamus palosverdesensis)
4	E	Butterfly, Saint Francis' satyr (Neonympha mitchellii francisci)
1	E	Butterfly, San Bruno elfin (Callophrys mossii bayensis)
4	E	Butterfly, Schaus swallowtail (Heraclides (=Papilio) aristodemus ponceanus)
1	E	Butterfly, Smith's blue (Euphilotes enoptes smithi)
6	E	Butterfly, Uncompahgre fritillary (Boloria acrocnema)
3	E	Dragonfly, Hine's emerald (Somatochlora hineana)
1	E	Fly, Delhi Sands flower-loving (Rhaphiomidas terminatus abdominalis)
1	T	Moth, Kern primrose sphinx (Euproserpinus euterpe)
1	T	Naucorid, Ash Meadows (Ambrysus amargosus)
6	T	Skipper, Pawnee montane (Hesperia leonardus (=pawnee) montana)

Arachnids

Region	Status	Species
2	E	Harvestman, Bee Creek Cave (Texella reddelli)
2	E	Harvestman, Bone Cave (Texella reyesi)
2	E	Pseudoscorpion, Tooth Cave (Microcreagris texana)
4	E	Spider, spruce-fir moss (Microhexura montivaga)
2	E	Spider, Tooth Cave (Leptoneta myopica)

Crustaceans

Region	Status	Species
5	E	Amphipod, Hay's Spring (Stygobromus hayi)
4	E	Crayfish, cave [no common name] (Cambarus aculabrum)
4	E	Crayfish, cave [no common name] (Cambarus zophonastes)
4	E	Crayfish, Nashville (Orconectes shoupi)
1	E	Crayfish, Shasta (=placid) (Pacifastacus fortis)
1	E	Fairy shrimp, Conservancy (Branchinecta conservatio)
1	E	Fairy shrimp, longhorn (Branchinecta longiantenna)
1	E	Fairy shrimp, riverside (Streptocephalus woottoni)
1	T	Fairy shrimp, vernal pool (Branchinecta lynchi)
5	E	Isopod, Lee County cave (Lirceus usdagalun)
5	T	Isopod, Madison Cave (Antrolana lira)
2	E	Isopod, Socorro (Thermosphaeroma (=Exosphaeroma) thermophilus)
4	E	Shrimp, Alabama cave (Palaemonias alabamae)
1	E	Shrimp, California freshwater (Syncaris pacifica)
4	E	Shrimp, Kentucky cave (Palaemonias ganteri)
4	T	Shrimp, Squirrel Chimney Cave (=Florida cave) (Palaemonetes cummingi)
1	E	Tadpole shrimp, vernal pool (Lepidurus packardi)

FLOWERING PLANTS

Region	Status	Species
2	E	Large-fruited sand-verbena (Abronia macrocarpa)
1	E	Abutilon eremitopetalum (Plant, no common name)
1	E	Ko`oloa`ula (Abutilon menziesii)
1	E	Abutilon sandwicense (Plant, no common name)
1	E	Liliwai (Acaena exigua)
1	E	San Mateo thornmint (Acanthomintha obovata ssp. duttonii)
1	E	Round-leaved chaff-flower (Achyranthes splendens var. rotundata)
3	T	Northern wild monkshood (Aconitum noveboracense)
4	T	Sensitive joint-vetch (Aeschynomene virginica)
5	E	Sandplain gerardia (Agalinis acuta)
2	E	Arizona agave (Agave arizonica)
1	E	Mahoe (Alectryon macrococcus)
1	E	Alsinidendron obovatum (Plant, no common name)
1	E	Alsinidendron trinerve (Plant, no common name)
4	T	Seabeach amaranth (Amaranthus pumilus)
2	E	South Texas ambrosia (Ambrosia cheiranthifolia)
4	E	Crenulate lead-plant (Amorpha crenulata)
4	T	Little amphianthus (Amphianthus pusillus)
1	E	Large-flowered fiddleneck (Amsinckia grandiflora)
2	E	Kearney's blue-star (Amsonia kearneyana)
2	E	Tobusch fishhook cactus (Ancistrocactus tobuschii)
3	T	Price's potato-bean (Apios priceana)
1	E	McDonald's rock-cress (Arabis mcdonaldiana)
4	E	Rock cress (Arabis perstellata)
5	E	Shale barren rock-cress (Arabis serotina)
6	E	Dwarf bear-poppy (Arctomecon humilis)
1	E	Presidio (=Raven's) manzanita (Arctostaphylos hookeri var. ravenii)
1	T	Morro manzanita (Arctostaphylos morroensis)
4	E	Cumberland sandwort (Arenaria cumberlandensis)
1	E	Marsh sandwort (Arenaria paludicola)
2	E	Sacramento prickly-poppy (Argemone pleiacantha ssp. pinnatisecta)
1	E	Ka`u silversword (Argyroxiphium kauense)
1	E	`Ahinahina (=Haleakala silversword) (Argyroxiphium sandwicense ssp. macrocephalum)
1	E	`Ahinahina (=Mauna Kea silversword) (Argyroxiphium sandwicense ssp. sandwicense)
4	E	Aristida chaseae (Plant, no common name)
4	E	Pelos del diablo (Aristida portoricensis)
3	T	Mead's milkweed (Asclepias meadii)
6	T	Welsh's milkweed (Asclepias welshii)
4	E	Four-petal pawpaw (Asimina tetramera)
1	E	Cushenbury milk-vetch (Astragalus albens)
1	E	Applegate's milk-vetch (Astragalus applegatei)
4	E	Pyne's (=Guthrie's) ground-plum (Astragalus bibullatus)
2	E	Sentry milk-vetch (Astragalus cremnophylax var. cremnophylax)
2	E	Mancos milk-vetch (Astragalus humillimus)
6	T	Heliotrope milk-vetch (Astragalus montii)
6	E	Osterhout milk-vetch (Astragalus osterhoutii)
1	T	Ash Meadows milk-vetch (Astragalus phoenix)
5	E	Jesup's milk-vetch (Astragalus robbinsii var. jesupi)
2	E	Star cactus (Astrophytum asterias)
4	E	Auerodendron pauciflorum (Plant, no common name)
2	E	Texas ayenia (Ayenia limitaris)

Region	Status	Species
4	E	Palo de Ramón (Banara vanderbiltii)
4	E	Hairy rattleweed (Baptisia arachnifera)
1	E	Truckee barberry (Berberis sonnei)
5	T	Virginia round-leaf birch (Betula uber)
1	E	Ko`oko`olau (Bidens micrantha ssp. kalealaha)
1	E	Ko`oko`olau (Bidens wiebkei)
1	E	Sonoma sunshine (=Baker's stickyseed) (Blennosperma bakeri)
3	T	Decurrent false aster (Boltonia decurrens)
4	T	Florida bonamia (Bonamia grandiflora)
1	E	Bonamia menziesii (Plant, no common name)
1	E	`Olulu (Brighamia insignis)
1	E	Pua `ala (Brighamia rockii)
4	E	Vahl's boxwood (Buxus vahlii)
1	E	Uhiuhi (Caesalpinia kavaiense)
4	E	Capá rosa (=péndula cimarrona) (Callicarpa ampla)
2	E	Texas poppy-mallow (Callirhoe scabriuscula)
1	T	Tiburon mariposa lily (Calochortus tiburonensis)
1	E	Calyptranthes thomasiana (Plant, no common name)
4	T	Palma de manaca or manac palm (Calyptronoma rivalis)
1	T	San Benito evening-primrose (Camissonia benitensis)
4	E	Brooksville (=Robins') bellflower (Campanula robinsiae)
1	E	`Awikiwiki (Canavalia molokaiensis)
4	E	Small-anthered bittercress (Cardamine micrantha)
2	T	Navajo sedge (Carex specuicola)
1	E	Tiburon paintbrush (Castilleja affinis ssp. neglecta)
1	E	San Clemente Island Indian paintbrush (Castilleja grisea)
1	E	California jewelflower (Caulanthus californicus)
1	E	Coyote ceanothus (=Coyote Valley California-lilac) (Ceanothus ferrisae)
1	T	Spring-loving centaury (Centaurium namophilum)
1	E	`Awiwi (Centaurium sebaeoides)
4	E	Fragrant prickly-apple (Cereus eriophorus var. fragrans)
4	E	Chamaecrista glandulosa var. mirabilis (=Cassia mirabilis) (Plant, no common name)
4	E	Deltoid spurge (Chamaesyce deltoidea ssp. deltoidea)
1	E	`Akoko (Chamaesyce deppeana (=Euphorbia d.))
4	T	Garber's spurge (Chamaesyce garberi)
1	E	`Ewa Plains `akoko (Chamaesyce skottsbergii var. kalaeloana)
1	E	`Akoko (Chamaesyce celastroides var. kaenana)
1	E	Chamaesyce halemanui (Plant, no common name)
1	E	`Akoko (Chamaesyce kuwaleana)
4	E	Pygmy fringe-tree (Chionanthus pygmaeus)
1	E	Howell's spineflower (Chorizanthe howellii)
1	E	Ben Lomond spineflower (Chorizanthe pungens var. hartwegiana)
1	T	Monterey spineflower (Chorizanthe pungens var. pungens)
1	E	Robust spineflower (includes Scotts Valley spineflower) (Chorizanthe robusta)
1	E	Sonoma spineflower (Chorizanthe valida)
4	E	Florida golden aster (Chrysopsis floridana)
1	E	Fountain thistle (Cirsium fontinale var. fontinale)
1	E	Chorro Creek bog thistle (Cirsium fontinale obispoense)
3	T	Pitcher's thistle (Cirsium pitcheri)
2	T	Sacramento Mountains thistle (Cirsium vinaceum)
1	E	Presidio clarkia (Clarkia franciscana)
1	E	Pismo clarkia (Clarkia speciosa immaculata)
4	E	Morefield's leather-flower (Clematis morefieldii)
4	E	Alabama leather-flower (Clematis socialis)
1	E	`Oha wai (Clermontia lindseyana)
1	E	`Oha wai (Clermontia oblongifolia ssp. brevipes)
1	E	`Oha wai (Clermontia oblongifolia ssp. mauiensis)
1	E	`Oha wai (Clermontia peleana)
1	E	`Oha wai (Clermontia pyrularia)
4	T	Pigeon wings (Clitoria fragrans)
1	E	Kauila (Colubrina oppositifolia)
4	E	Short-leaved rosemary (Conradina brevifolia)
4	E	Etonia rosemary (Conradina etonia)
4	E	Apalachicola rosemary (Conradina glabra)
4	T	Cumberland rosemary (Conradina verticillata)
1	E	Salt marsh bird's-beak (Cordylanthus maritimus ssp. maritimus)
1	E	Palmate-bracted bird's-beak (Cordylanthus palmatus)
1	E	Pennell's bird's-beak (Cordylanthus tenuis ssp. capillaris)
4	E	Palo de nigua (=capá jugüerilla) (Cornutia obovata)
2	T	Cochise pincushion cactus (Coryphantha (=Escobaria) robbinsorum)
2	E	Nellie cory cactus (Coryphantha (=Escobaria) minima)
2	T	Bunched cory cactus (Coryphantha ramillosa)
2	E	Pima pineapple cactus (Coryphantha scheeri var. robustispina)
2	T	Lee pincushion cactus (Coryphantha sneedii var. leei)
2	E	Sneed pincushion cactus (Coryphantha sneedii var. sneedii)
4	E	Cranichis ricartii (Plant, no common name)
4	E	Higuero de Sierra (Crescentia portoricensis)
4	E	Avon Park harebells (Crotalaria avonensis)
2	E	Terlingua Creek cats-eye (Cryptantha crassipes)
4	E	Okeechobee gourd (Cucurbita okeechobeensis ssp. okeechobeensis)
1	E	Haha (Cyanea asarifolia)
1	E	Haha (Cyanea copelandii ssp. copelandii)
1	E	Haha (Cyanea grimesiana ssp. obatae)
1	E	Haha (Cyanea hamatiflora ssp. carlsonii)
1	E	Haha (Cyanea lobata)
1	E	Cyanea macrostegia ssp. gibsonii (Plant, no common name)
1	E	Haha (Cyanea mannii)
1	E	Haha (Cyanea mceldowneyi)
1	E	Haha (Cyanea pinnatifida)
1	E	Haha (Cyanea procera)
1	E	Haha (Cyanea shipmannii)
1	E	Haha (Cyanea stictophylla)
1	E	Cyanea superba (Plant, no common name)
1	E	Haha (Cyanea truncata)
1	E	Cyanea undulata (Plant, no common name)
2	T	Jones cycladenia (Cycladenia humilis var. jonesii)
1	E	Ha`iwale (Cyrtandra crenata)
1	E	Ha`iwale (Cyrtandra giffardii)
1	T	Ha`iwale (Cyrtandra limahuliensis)
1	E	Ha`iwale (Cyrtandra munroi)
1	E	Ha`iwale (Cyrtandra polyantha)
1	E	Ha`iwale (Cyrtandra tintinnabula)
3	E	Leafy prairie-clover (Dalea (=Petalostemum) foliosa)
4	E	Daphnopsis hellerana (Plant, no common name)
4	E	Beautiful pawpaw (Deeringothamnus pulchellus)
4	E	Rugel's pawpaw (Deeringothamnus rugelii)
1	E	Delissea rhytidosperma (Plant, no common name)
1	E	San Clemente Island larkspur (Delphinium variegatum ssp. kinkiense)
4	E	Garrett's mint (Dicerandra christmanii)
4	E	Longspurred mint (Dicerandra cornutissima)
4	E	Scrub mint (Dicerandra frutescens)
4	E	Lakela's mint (Dicerandra immaculata)
1	E	Slender-horned spineflower (Dodecahema leptoceras)
1	E	Na`ena`e (Dubautia herbstobatae)
1	E	Dubautia latifolia (Plant, no common name)
1	E	Dubautia pauciflorula (Plant, no common name)
1	E	Santa Clara Valley dudleya (Dudleya setchellii)
1	E	Santa Barbara Island liveforever (Dudleya traskiae)
4	E	Smooth coneflower (Echinacea laevigata)
4	E	Tennessee purple coneflower (Echinacea tennesseensis)
2	E	Nichol's Turk's head cactus (Echinocactus horizonthalonius var. nicholii)
2	T	Chisos Mountain hedgehog cactus (Echinocereus chisoensis var. chisoensis)
2	E	Kuenzler hedgehog cactus (Echinocereus fendleri var. kuenzleri)
2	E	Lloyd's hedgehog cactus (Echinocereus lloydii)
2	E	Black lace cactus (Echinocereus reichenbachii (=melanocentrus) var. albertii)
2	E	Arizona hedgehog cactus (Echinocereus triglochidiatus var. arizonicus)
2	E	Davis' green pitaya (Echinocereus viridiflorus var. davisii)
2	T	Lloyd's Mariposa cactus (Echinomastus (=Sclerocactus) mariposensis)
1	T	Ash Meadows sunray (Enceliopsis nudicaulis var. corrugata)
1	E	Kern mallow (Eremalche kernensis)
1	E	Santa Ana River woolly-star (Eriastrum densifolium ssp. sanctorum)
1	T	Hoover's woolly-star (Eriastrum hooveri)
6	E	Maguire daisy (Erigeron maguirei var. maguirei)
1	T	Parish's daisy (Erigeron parishii)
2	T	Zuni (=rhizome) fleabane (Erigeron rhizomatus)
1	E	Indian Knob mountain balm (Eriodictyon altissimum)
2	T	Gypsum wild-buckwheat (Eriogonum gypsophilum)
4	T	Scrub buckwheat (Eriogonum longifolium var. gnaphalifolium)
1	E	Cushenbury buckwheat (Eriogonum ovalifolium var. vineum)
1	E	Steamboat buckwheat (Eriogonum ovalifolium var. williamsiae)
6	E	Clay-loving wild-buckwheat (Eriogonum pelinophilum)
1	E	San Mateo woolly sunflower (Eriophyllum latilobum)
1	E	San Diego button-celery (Eryngium aristulatum var. parishii)
1	E	Loch Lomond coyote-thistle (Eryngium constancei)
4	E	Snakeroot (Eryngium cuneifolium)
1	E	Contra Costa wallflower (Erysimum capitatum var. angustatum)
1	E	Menzies' wallflower (Erysimum menziesii)
1	E	Ben Lomond wallflower (Erysimum teretifolium)

Region	Status	Species
3	E	Minnesota trout lily (Erythronium propullans)
4	E	Uvillo (Eugenia haematocarpa)
1	E	Nioi (Eugenia koolauensis)
4	E	Eugenia woodburyana (Plant, no common name)
4	T	Telephus spurge (Euphorbia telephioides)
6	T	Penland alpine fen mustard (Eutrema penlandii)
1	E	Heau (Exocarpos luteolus)
1	E	Mehamehame (Flueggea neowawraea)
2	E	Johnston's frankenia (Frankenia johnstonii)
1	E	Gahnia lanaiensis (Plant, no common name)
4	E	Small's milkpea (Galactia smallii)
1	E	Na`u or Hawaiian gardenia (Gardenia brighamii)
3	T	Geocarpon minimum (Plant, no common name)
1	E	Hawaiian red-flowered geranium (Geranium arboreum)
1	E	Nohoanu (Geranium multiflorum)
4	T	Gesneria pauciflora (Plant, no common name)
4	E	Spreading avens (Geum radiatum)
1	E	Monterey gilia (Gilia tenuiflora ssp. arenaria)
4	E	Beautiful goetzea or matabuey (Goetzea elegans)
1	E	Gouania hillebrandii (Plant, no common name)
1	E	Gouania meyenii (Plant, no common name)
1	E	Gouania vitifolia (Plant, no common name)
1	T	Ash Meadows gumplant (Grindelia fraxino-pratensis)
1	E	Haplostachys haplostachya (Plant, no common name)
4	E	Harper's beauty (Harperocallis flava)
4	T	Higo chumbo (Harrisia portoricensis)
2	E	Todsen's pennyroyal (Hedeoma todsenii)
1	E	`Awiwi (Hedyotis cookiana)
1	E	Kio`ele (Hedyotis coriacea)
1	E	Hedyotis degeneri (Plant, no common name)
1	E	Pilo (Hedyotis mannii)
1	E	Hedyotis parvula (Plant, no common name)
4	E	Roan Mountain bluet (Hedyotis purpurea var. montana)
1	E	Na Pali beach hedyotis (Hedyotis st.-johnii)
4	E	Schweinitz's sunflower (Helianthus schweinitzii)
5	T	Swamp pink (Helonias bullata)
1	T	Marin dwarf-flax (Hesperolinon congestum)
1	E	Hesperomannia arborescens (Plant, no common name)
1	E	Hesperomannia arbuscula (Plant, no common name)
1	E	Hesperomannia lydgatei (Plant, no common name)
4	T	Dwarf-flowered heartleaf (Hexastylis naniflora)
1	E	Kauai hau kuahiwi (Hibiscadelphus distans)
1	E	Koki`o ke`oke`o (Hibiscus arnottianus ssp. immaculatus)
1	E	Ma`o hau hele (Hibiscus brackenridgei)
1	E	Clay's hibiscus (Hibiscus clayi)
2	E	Slender rush-pea (Hoffmannseggia tenella)
6	T	Water howellia (Howellia aquatilis)
4	T	Mountain golden heather (Hudsonia montana)
3	E	Lakeside daisy (Hymenoxys herbacea)
2	E	Texas prairie dawn-flower (=Texas bitterweed) (Hymenoxys texana)
4	E	Highlands scrub hypericum (Hypericum cumulicola)
4	E	Cook's holly (Ilex cookii)
4	E	Ilex sintenisii (Plant, no common name)
5	E	Peter's Mountain mallow (Iliamna corei)
2	E	Holy Ghost ipomopsis (Ipomopsis sancti-spiritus)
3	E	Dwarf lake iris (Iris lacustris)
1	E	Hilo ischaemum (Ischaemum byrone)
1	E	Aupaka (Isodendrion hosakae)
1	E	Wahine noho kula (Isodendrion pyrifolium)
3	T	Small whorled pogonia (Isotria medeoloides)
1	T	Ash Meadows ivesia (Ivesia kingii var. eremica)
4	E	Beach jacquemontia (Jacquemontia reclinata)
1	E	Cooley's water-willow (Justicia cooleyi)
1	E	Cooke's koki`o (Kokia cookei)
1	E	Koki`o (=hau-hele`ula or Hawaii tree cotton) (Kokia drynarioides)
1	E	Kamakahala (Labordia lydgatei)
1	E	Burke's goldfields (Lasthenia burkei)
1	E	Beach layia (Layia carnosa)
1	E	San Joaquin wooly-threads (Lembertia congdonii)
4	E	Lepanthes eltoroensis (Plant, no common name)
6	E	Barneby ridge-cress (=peppercress) (Lepidium barnebyanum)
4	E	Leptocereus grantianus (Plant, no common name)
3	T	Prairie bush-clover (Lespedeza leptostachya)
6	T	Dudley Bluffs bladderpod (Lesquerella congesta)
3	E	Missouri bladderpod (Lesquerella filiformis)
1	E	San Bernardino Mountains bladderpod (Lesquerella kingii ssp. bernardina)
4	T	Lyrate bladderpod (Lesquerella lyrata)
2	E	White bladderpod (Lesquerella pallida)
6	E	Kodachrome bladderpod (Lesquerella tumulosa)
4	T	Heller's blazingstar (Liatris helleri)
4	E	Scrub blazingstar (Liatris ohlingerae)
1	E	Western lily (Lilium occidental)
1	E	Butte County meadowfoam (Limnanthes floccosa ssp. californica)
1	E	Sebastopol meadowfoam (Limnanthes vinculans)
3	E	Pondberry (Lindera melissifolia)
1	E	Nehe (Lipochaeta fauriei)
1	E	Nehe (Lipochaeta kamolensis)
1	E	Nehe (Lipochaeta lobata var. leptophylla)
1	E	Nehe (Lipochaeta micrantha)
1	E	Nehe (Lipochaeta tenuifolia)
1	E	Lipochaeta venosa (Plant, no common name)
1	E	Nehe (Lipochaeta waimeaensis)
1	E	Lobelia niihauensis (Plant, no common name)
1	E	Lobelia oahuensis (Plant, no common name)
1	E	Bradshaw's desert-parsley (=lomatium) (Lomatium bradshawii)
1	E	San Clemente Island broom (Lotus dendroideus ssp. traskiae)
4	E	Scrub lupine (Lupinus aridorum)
1	E	Clover lupine (Lupinus tidestromii)
4	E	Lyonia truncata var. proctorii (Plant, no common name)
4	E	Rough-leaved loosestrife (Lysimachia asperulaefolia)
1	E	Lysimachia filifolia (Plant, no common name)
1	E	Lysimachia lydgatei (Plant, no common name)
4	T	White birds-in-a-nest (Macbridea alba)
1	E	San Clemente Island bush-mallow (Malacothamnus clementinus)
2	E	Walker's manioc (Manihot walkerae)
1	E	Mariscus fauriei (Plant, no common name)
1	E	Mariscus pennatiformis (Plant, no common name)
4	T	Mohr's Barbara's buttons (Marshallia mohrii)
1	E	Alani (Melicope lydgatei)
1	E	Alani (Melicope mucronulata)
1	E	Alani (Melicope adscendens)
1	E	Alani (Melicope balloui)
1	E	Alani (Melicope haupuensis)
1	E	Alani (Melicope knudsenii)
1	E	Alani (Melicope ovalis)
1	E	Alani (Melicope pallida)
1	E	Alani (Melicope quadrangularis)
1	E	Alani (Melicope reflexa)
1	T	Ash Meadows blazing-star (Mentzelia leucophylla)
3	E	Michigan monkey-flower (Mimulus glabratus var. michiganensis)
1	E	MacFarlane's four-o'clock (Mirabilis macfarlanei)
4	E	Mitracarpus maxwelliae (no common name)
4	E	Mitracarpus polycladus (no common name)
1	E	Munroidendron racemosum (no common name)
4	E	Myrcia paganii (no common name)
1	E	Neraudia angulata (Plant, no common name)
1	E	Neraudia sericea (Plant, no common name)
1	E	Amargosa niterwort (Nitrophila mohavensis)
4	E	Britton's beargrass (Nolina brittoniana)
1	E	`Aiea (Nothocestrum breviflorum)
1	E	`Aiea (Nothocestrum peltatum)
1	E	Kulu`i (Nototrichium humile)
1	E	Holei (Ochrosia kilaueaensis)
1	E	Eureka Valley evening-primrose (Oenothera avita ssp. eurekensis)
1	E	Antioch Dunes evening-primrose (Oenothera deltoides ssp. howellii)
1	E	Bakersfield cactus (Opuntia treleasei)
1	E	California Orcutt grass (Orcuttia californica)
4	E	Palo de rosa (Ottoschulzia rhodoxylon)
4	E	Canby's dropwort (Oxypolis canbyi)
1	E	Cushenbury oxytheca (Oxytheca parishii var. goodmaniana)
3	T	Fassett's locoweed (Oxytropis campestris var. chartacea)
1	F	Carter's panicgrass (Panicum fauriei var. carteri)
4	T	Papery whitlow-wort (Paronychia chartacea)
5	F	Furbish lousewort (Pedicularis furbishiae)
2	T	Siler pincushion cactus (Pediocactus sileri)
2	E	Peebles Navajo cactus (Pediocactus peeblesianus var. peeblesianus)
2	E	Brady pincushion cactus (Pediocactus bradyi)
2	E	Knowlton cactus (Pediocactus knowltonii)
6	E	San Rafael cactus (Pediocactus despainii)
6	E	Blowout penstemon (Penstemon haydenii)
6	E	Penland beardtongue (Penstemon penlandii)
1	E	White-rayed pentachaeta (Pentachaeta bellidiflora)
4	E	Wheeler's peperomia (Peperomia wheeleri)
1	T	Makou (Peucedanum sandwicense)
6	E	Clay phacelia (Phacelia argillacea)
6	E	North Park phacelia (Phacelia formosula)
2	E	Texas trailing phlox (Phlox nivalis ssp. texensis)
1	E	Phyllostegia glabra var. lanaiensis (Plant, no common name)
1	E	Phyllostegia mannii (Plant, no common name)
1	E	Phyllostegia mollis (Plant, no common name)
1	E	Phyllostegia waimeae (Plant, no common name)
6	T	Dudley Bluffs twinpod (Physaria obcordata)
4	E	Key tree-cactus (Pilosocereus robinii (=Cereus r.))
4	T	Godfrey's butterwort (Pinguicula ionantha)
4	E	Ruth's golden aster (Pityopsis (=Heterotheca =Chrysopsis) ruthii)
1	E	Laukahi kuahiwi (Plantago hawaiensis)
1	E	Laukahi kuahiwi (Plantago princeps)

region	status	species
3	T	Eastern prairie fringed orchid (Platanthera leucophaea)
2	T	Western prairie fringed orchid (Platanthera praeclara)
4	E	Chupacallos (=Chupagallo) (Pleodendron macranthum)
1	E	Mann's bluegrass (Poa mannii)
1	E	Hawaiian bluegrass (Poa sandvicensis)
1	E	Poa siphonoglossa (Plant, no common name)
1	E	San Diego mesa mint (Pogogyne abramsii)
1	E	Otay mesa mint (Pogogyne nudiuscula)
4	E	Lewton's polygala (Polygala lewtonii)
4	E	Tiny polygala (Polygala smallii)
4	E	Wireweed (Polygonella basiramia)
4	E	Sandlace (Polygonella myriophylla)
1	E	Po`e (Portulaca sclerocarpa)
2	E	Little Aguja pondweed (Potamogeton clystocarpus)
5	E	Robbins' cinquefoil (Potentilla robbinsiana)
6	T	Maguire primrose (Primula maguirei)
1	E	Loulu (Pritchardia affinis)
1	E	Loulu (Pritchardia munroi)
4	E	Scrub plum (Prunus geniculata)
1	E	Kaulu (Pteralyxia kauaiensis)
5	E	Harperella (Ptilimnium nodosum (=fluviatile))
2	E	Arizona cliffrose (Purshia subintegra)
2	T	Hinckley's oak (Quercus hinckleyi)
6	E	Autumn buttercup (Ranunculus acriformis var. aestivalis)
1	E	Remya kauaiensis (Plant, no common name)
1	E	Maui remya (Remya mauiensis)
1	E	Remya montgomeryi (Plant, no common name)
4	E	Chapman rhododendron (Rhododendron chapmanii)
4	E	Michaux's sumac (Rhus michauxii)
5	T	Knieskern's beaked-rush (Rhynchospora knieskernii)
4	E	Miccosukee gooseberry (Ribes echinellum)
1	E	Rollandia crispa (Plant, no common name)
1	E	Gambel's watercress (Rorippa gambellii)
4	E	Bunched arrowhead (Sagittaria fasciculata)
4	T	Kral's water-plantain (Sagittaria secundifolia)
1	E	Sanicula mariversa (Plant, no common name)
1	E	Lanai sandalwood or `iliahi (Santalum freycinetianum var. lanaiense)
4	E	Green pitcher-plant (Sarracenia oreophila)
4	E	Alabama canebrake pitcher-plant (Sarracenia rubra ssp. alabamensis)
4	E	Mountain sweet pitcher-plant (Sarracenia rubra ssp. jonesii)
1	E	Dwarf naupaka (Scaevola coriacea)
1	E	Diamond Head schiedea (Schiedea adamantis)
1	E	Ma`oli`oli (Schiedea apokremnos)
1	E	Schiedea haleakalensis (Plant, no common name)
1	E	Schiedea kaalae (Plant, no common name)
1	E	Schiedea lydgatei (Plant, no common name)
1	E	Schiedea spergulina var. leiopoda (Plant, no common name)
1	T	Schiedea spergulina var. spergulina (Plant, no common name)
6	E	Shrubby reed-mustard (=toad-flax cress) (Schoenocrambe suffrutescens)
6	T	Clay reed-mustard (Schoenocrambe argillacea)
6	E	Barneby reed-mustard (Schoenocrambe barnebyi)
4	T	Schoepfia arenaria (Plant, no common name)
4	E	American chaffseed (Schwalbea americana)
5	E	Northeastern (=Barbed bristle) bulrush (Scirpus ancistrochaetus)
2	T	Mesa Verde cactus (Sclerocactus mesae-verdae)
6	T	Uinta Basin hookless cactus (Sclerocactus glaucus)
6	E	Wright fishhook cactus (Sclerocactus wrightiae)
4	T	Florida skullcap (Scutellaria floridana)
4	E	Large-flowered skullcap (Scutellaria montana)
3	T	Leedy's roseroot (Sedum integrifolium ssp. leedyi)
2	T	San Francisco Peaks groundsel (Senecio franciscanus)
1	E	Hayun lagu (Guam), Tronkon guafi (Rota) (Serianthes nelsonii)
1	E	`Ohai (Sesbania tomentosa)
1	T	Nelson's checker-mallow (Sidalcea nelsoniana)
1	E	Pedate checker-mallow (Sidalcea pedata)
1	E	Silene alexandri (Plant, no common name)
1	T	Silene hawaiiensis (Plant, no common name)
1	E	Silene lanceolata (Plant, no common name)
1	E	Silene perlmanii (Plant, no common name)
4	E	Fringed campion (Silene polypetala)
4	E	White irisette (Sisyrinchium dichotomum)
4	E	Erubia (Solanum drymophilum)
1	E	Popolo ku mai (Solanum incompletum)
1	E	`Aiakeakua, popolo (Solanum sandwicense)
4	T	White-haired goldenrod (Solidago albopilosa)
3	T	Houghton's goldenrod (Solidago houghtonii)
4	E	Short's goldenrod (Solidago shortii)
4	T	Blue Ridge goldenrod (Solidago spithamaea)
1	E	Spermolepis hawaiiensis (Plant, no common name)
4	E	Gentian pinkroot (Spigelia gentianoides)
4	E	Virginia spiraea (Spiraea virginiana)
6	T	Ute ladies'-tresses (Spiranthes diluvialis)
2	E	Navasota ladies'-tresses (Spiranthes parksii)
4	T	Cóbana negra (Stahlia monosperma)
1	E	Stenogyne angustifolia (Plant, no common name)
1	E	Stenogyne bifida (Plant, no common name)
1	E	Stenogyne campanulata (Plant, no common name)
1	E	Stenogyne kanehoana (Plant, no common name)
1	E	Malheur wire-lettuce (Stephanomeria malheurensis)
1	E	Metcalf Canyon jewelflower (Streptanthus albidus ssp. albidus)
1	E	Tiburon jewelflower (Streptanthus niger)
4	E	Palo de jazmín (Styrax portoricensis)
2	E	Texas snowbells (Styrax texana)
1	E	California seablite (Suaeda californica)
1	E	Eureka Dune grass (Swallenia alexandrae)
4	E	Palo colorado (Ternstroemia luquillensis)
4	E	Ternstroemia subsessilis (Plant, no common name)
1	E	Tetramolopium arenarium (Plant, no common name)
1	E	Pamakani (Tetramolopium capillare)
1	E	Tetramolopium filiforme (Plant, no common name)
1	E	Tetramolopium lepidotum ssp. lepidotum (Plant, no common name)
1	E	Tetramolopium remyi (Plant, no common name)
1	T	Tetramolopium rockii (Plant, no common name)
1	E	`Ohe`ohe (Tetraplasandra gymnocarpa)
4	E	Cooley's meadowrue (Thalictrum cooleyi)
1	E	Slender-petaled mustard (Thelypodium stenopetalum)
2	E	Ashy dogweed (Thymophylla tephroleuca)
6	T	Last Chance townsendia (Townsendia aprica)
4	E	Bariaco (=guayabacón) (Trichilia triacantha)
3	E	Running buffalo clover (Trifolium stoloniferum)
4	E	Persistent trillium (Trillium persistens)
4	E	Relict trillium (Trillium reliquum)
1	E	Solano grass (Tuctoria mucronata)
1	E	Opuhe (Urera kaalae)
4	E	Vernonia proctorii (Plant, no common name)
1	E	Hawaiian vetch (Vicia menziesii)
1	E	Vigna o-wahuensis (Plant, no common name)
1	E	Pamakani (Viola chamissoniana chamissoniana)
1	E	Viola helenae (Plant, no common name)
1	E	Viola lanaiensis (Plant, no common name)
4	E	Wide-leaf warea (Warea amplexifolia)
4	E	Carter's mustard (Warea carteri)
1	E	Dwarf iliau (Wilkesia hobdyi)
1	E	Xylosma crenatum (Plant, no common name)
4	E	Tennessee yellow-eyed grass (Xyris tennesseensis)
1	E	A`e (Zanthoxylum hawaiiense)
4	E	St. Thomas prickly-ash (Zanthoxylum thomasianum)
2	E	Texas wild-rice (Zizania texana)
4	E	Florida ziziphus (Ziziphus celata)

NON-FLOWERING PLANTS

Conifers & Cycads

region	status	species
1	E	Santa Cruz cypress (Cupressus abramsiana)
4	E	Florida torreya (Torreya taxifolia)

Ferns & Allies

region	status	species
1	E	Pendant kihi fern (Adenophorus periens)
4	E	Adiantum vivesii (Fern, no common name)
3	T	American hart's-tongue fern (Asplenium scolopendrium var. americanum)
1	E	Asplenium fragile var. insulare (Fern, no common name)
1	E	Pauoa (Ctenitis squamigera)
4	E	Elfin tree fern (Cyathea dryopteroides)
1	E	Asplenium-leaved diellia (Diellia erecta)
1	E	Diellia falcata (Fern, no common name)
1	E	Diellia pallida (Fern, no common name)
1	E	Diellia unisora (Fern, no common name)
1	E	Diplazium molokaiense (Fern, no common name)
4	E	Elaphoglossum serpens (Fern, no common name)
1	E	Wawae`iole (Huperzia mannii)
1	E	Louisiana quillwort (Isoetes louisianensis)
4	E	Black-spored quillwort (Isoetes melanospora)
4	E	Mat-forming quillwort (Isoetes tegetiformans)
1	E	Wawae`iole (Lycopodium nutans)
1	E	`Ihi`ihi (Marsilea villosa)
7	E	Aleutian shield-fern (=Aleutian holly-fern) (Polystichum aleuticum)
4	E	Polystichum calderonense (Fern, no common name)
1	E	Pteris lidgatei (Fern, no common name)
4	E	Tectaria estremerana (Fern, no common name)
4	T	Alabama streak-sorus fern (Thelypteris pilosa var. alabamensis)
4	E	Thelypteris inabonensis (Fern, no common name)
4	E	Thelypteris verecunda (Fern, no common name)
4	E	Thelypteris yaucoensis (Fern, no common name)

Lichens

region	status	species
4	E	Florida perforate cladonia (Cladonia perforata)
4	E	Rock gnome lichen (Gymnoderma lineare)

KEY LARGO COTTON MOUSE
Survival of this endangered rodent hinges on preserving the hardwood forests of Key Largo, Florida.

INDEX

bold indicates illustration

Adams, Mt., Wash. **76**
Alani 123
Alligator River N.W.R., N.C. 115
Alligators 107-108; Florida 131
Amaral, Michael 122
Aransas N.W.R., Tex. 19
Ash Meadows milkvetchs **90-91,** 91
Ashy dogweeds 37
Audubon, John James 119
Audubon Society, National 18
Auks, great 139

Babbitt, Bruce 26, 142
Bayles, David 139
Bears, grizzly 19, 108-112, 114-115, 116, 119; California 117, **117;** golden 17
Beatty, Nev. 132
Beetles 118-122; American burying 66, **67,** 118-122; northeastern beach tiger 122; Puritan tiger 122; wood-boring **49**
Bighorns, badlands 107
Bison 17, 18, 104; skulls **104**
Blackfin cisco 131
Block Island, R.I. 119, 120-122
Bob Marshall Wilderness (area), Mont. 110, 111, 113
Bonneville Dam, Oreg.-Wash. 77, **77, 82-83**
Boyd, Diane 115
Briggs, Gary 138
Buffalo *see* Bison
Butterflies 125; El Segundo blue **54,** 55; Morpho 125

Cacti 36
California Desert Protection Act (1994) 136
Caribou, woodland 17
Carson, Rachel: quoted 8
Center for Plant Conservation 140
Chickens, prairie 120
Christy, Dick 109-110
Clark County, Nev. 135-137
Clinton, Bill 23, 25, 136
Columbia River and Basin, Canada-U.S. 77, **77,** 82, **82-83,** 138-140
Condors, California **6-7,** 7, 50, **50-51,** 119, 130; chick **160**
Coneflowers 126; purple 126; smooth 126; Tennessee purple 126
Convention on International Trade in Endangered Species (CITES) (1973) 21
Cougars 36, 114, 115
Cranes: sandhill 19, 65; "whoophill" **65;** whooping 10, **10-11,** 19, **64-65,** 65, 119
Crayfish, Shasta 36
Crocodiles, American 19, 102, **102,** 108

Daces, Ash Meadows speckled 91, **91**
The Dalles Dam, Wash. 77, **77**
Dams 28, 56, 82, 139; Bonneville 77, **82-83;** The Dalles 77, **77;** Tellico 44, **44,** 127
Darters: sharphead 127; snail 44, **44-45,** 127-128
Darwin, Charles: quoted 5
DDT 19, 26, 28
Deer, Florida Key 102, **103**
Defenders of Wildlife (environmental group) 113

Denali N.P., Alas. 114
Desert Southwest (region), U.S. **86-93**
Desert Tortoise Conservation Center 93
Desert Tortoise Reserve 135
Desert Wildlife Management Areas 136-137
Dickens, Elizabeth 120, 121
Dodge, Earl 120
Doves, mourning **66-67**
Duffield, John 115

Eagles, bald 2, **2-3,** 19, 26, 28, 119, 158, **158-159**
Earth Day 20
Ecosystem management 140-143
Edison's St. John's-wort **101**
Elephants 21
Endangered and threatened species: apparel made from 21, 56, 120, 124, 141; chart of U.S. species 28-37; inbreeding 41, 131-132; list of U.S. species 146-152; long range planning 140-143; rate of extinction 17; revisions to list 72; tourism relating to 107, 115; wildfire regeneration 130
Endangered Species Act (ESA) of 1973: amendments to 25-26, 110; content of bill 22-23, 110, 122; creation of 20; first insect species listed 123; funding of 24; opposition to 23-24, 110, 113, 123, 136-137; status of listed species 133
Endangered Species Preservation Act of 1966 20
Etnier, Dave 127
Everglades N.P., Fla. 98, 102

Falcons: northern aplomado 28; peregrine 19, 26
Federal Environmental Pesticide Control Act (1972) 20
Federal Land Policy Management Act 140
Ferrets, black-footed **42,** 43, **43,** 130-131
Flies, Delhi Sands flower-loving 123
Florida **94-103**
Florida perforate cladonia 123
Franklinia trees 127
Frogs, California red-legged 25
Furbish louseworts 127

Gambusia, amistad 135
Gap analysis 140-143
Ghiradella, Helen 125
Gifford Pinchot N.F., Wash. 77, **77**
Glacier N.P., Mont. 110, 112
Gnatcatchers, coastal California 86, 91, **91,** 142
Goshawks, northern 137
Grasses, cutthroat **101**
Grasso, Michelle 136
Guayules 126

Habitat Conservation Plan (HCP) 135-137
Haldane, J.B.S. 118
Haneberry, Lou 131
Hau Kuahiwi 125
Henry, Gary 115
Hens, heath 113, 120
Hoff, Karen 132
Hugo, Victor: quoted 10
Humboldt County, Calif.: logging **73-74**

Indians of North America: Cherokee creation myth 127; Nez Perce wolf ceremony 113; use of coneflowers 126
International Whaling Commission 107
Ivie, Mike 118
Ivory 21

Jays, Florida scrub 60, **61**

Kangaroo rats, Stephens' 123
Kites, Everglade snail 119
Klickitat River, Wash. **84-85**
Knowlton cacti 36
Kozol, Andrea 121
Kwiatkowski, Don 130-131

Lacey Act 20, 21
Lake Placid scrub mints 142
Lake Wales Ridge N.W.R., Fla. 101, 142-143
Leeches 126
Leopold, Aldo 118
Lewis, Bill 120
Lewis, Keith 120
Lewis, Robert 120
Lions, mountain *see* Cougars
Lizards, San Diego coast horned **55**
Loetscher, Ila **53**
Loew, Brian 123
Los Angeles, Calif. 86, **88-89,** 89
Los Padres N.F., Calif. **50**
Lumber industry 74, 129, 137, 138; clear cut logging 77, **78-79,** 139, 140; logging **80**

Madel, Mike 110
Madtoms, Scioto 37
Mahoe **16,** 17
Mallows 130
Manatees, West Indian(=Florida) 8, **8-9,** 68, **68-69**
Marincovich, Jack 138
Marine Mammal Protection Act 20, 72, 106
Marlow, Ron 134, 135
Marshall, Robert: quoted 111
Martha's Vineyard, Mass. 113, 122
Matthews, Tom 141-142
Meeteetse, Wyo. 130, 131
Mice: Florida 143; Key Largo cotton **153**
Mojave Desert, Calif.-Nev. 134-137
Mollusks 28, 124-125; see also Mussels
Mosquitoes 37, 96
Moths, army cutworm 111
Murphy, Terry 137
Murrelets, marbled 137
Mussels 28, 124-125; Cumberland combshell 57; fanshell 56, **56-57;** pocketbook 124; shiny pigtoe 124; Wabash riffleshells 115; zebra 125

National Audubon Society 18
National Biological Service 25
National Biological Survey 124
The Nature Conservancy 91, 120, 124, 140, 143; Block Island chapter 122
Nellie Cory cacti 36
Nene 27, **27**
Neves, Dick 124, 126
1918 Federal Migratory Bird Treaty Act 20
Northern Continental Divide Ecosystem (NCDE) 109-115

Oak scrubs, Florida 142-143
Ocelots 36
Olympic Peninsula, Wash. **78-79**
Orange County, Calif. **88-89,** 141-142
Orcutt's spineflowers 142
Otters, southern sea 106-107
Owls, northern spotted 74, 77, 80, **80-81,** 137, 138

Pacific Northwest (region), U.S. **76-85**
Pacific Rivers Council 139
Pacific yews 137
Panthers: Florida 41, **41,** 95, 131; see also Cougars
Parakeets, Carolina 119-120, 141
Pelicans, brown 28, 72
Perforate reindeer moss **101**
Pesticides 48, 50, 95, 96, 131-132; DDT 19-20, 26, 28; Federal Environmental Pesticide Control Act (1972) 20; sprayed over Fort Myers, Fl. **96-97**

Peter's Mountain mallows 130
Pigeons, passenger 17, 38, **38,** 119
Pike, blue 109
Plovers, piping 122
Po'e 34
President's Forest Plan 138, 140
Pupfish, Devil's Hole 119

Raithel, Chris 121
Raithel, John 121
Ravens 135
Red Rock Lakes N.W.R., Mont. 18
Reed, Nathaniel 141
Riparian zones 132
Roosevelt, Theodore 94; quoted 2, 139
Rubber plants 125

Salamanders: red-backed 36; Shenandoah 36
Salmon 74, 76, 77, 138-140; chinook 139; chinook smolts 84, **84;** coho 138; sockeye 139
San Diego mesa-mint 119
Scott, Mike 140-141
Scrub paw-paws 142
Sea lions, Steller **46-47,** 47
"Seal Treaty" (1911) 20
Selway-Bitterroot wilderness, Idaho-Mont. 116
Semaphore cacti **100,** 101
Servheen, Chris 109
Shen-Miller, Jane 126
Snake River, U.S. 139
Snakes, indigo 143

Southwest (region), U.S.: threats to species habitats 86, **86-87**
Sparrows: dusky seaside 121, 130; Santa Barbara song 137
Storks, wood 95, 98, **98-99**
Sturgeons, pallid 140
Swans, southern trumpeter 18

Tadpole shrimp, vernal pool **62-63,** 63
Tellico Dam, Tenn. 44, **44,** 127
Terns, least 122
Thaxton, Jon 60, **61**
Thismia Americanus 119
Thoreau, Henry David: quoted 7
Toads: amargosa 132, 135; Wyoming **70-71,** 71
Tortoises: desert 86, **92-93,** 134-136; gopher 143
Trinko, Mark 136-137
Tropical rosy periwinkles 126
Trout: bull 140; silver 111; westslope cutthroat 140
Turner, John 140
Turtles: green sea 52, **52;** sea 36, 52
Twain, Mark 25, 76

U.S. Congress 18-22, 24-25, 44, 106, 127
U.S. Fish and Wildlife Service 21, 25, 91, 108, 130, 135; grizzly bear recovery 109; land acquisition 143; wolf reintroduction 113, 115-116
U.S. Forest Service 140

Webb, Walter Prescott 87
Western prairie fringed orchids 48, **48-49,** 119
Whales: Atlantic gray 133; California gray 107; gray 72, **72-73;** Pacific gray 133; tourism relating to 107
Wilson, Alexander 119
Wolkoff, Dennis 122
Wolves 36; Florida red 143; gray 112-114; Mexican 116; red **4-5,** 5, **58-59,** 59, 115; tourism relating to 115
Woodpeckers, ivory-billed 129, **129,** 133

Yellowstone N.P., U.S. 108, 111, 112, 115

ACKNOWLEDGMENTS

DC: The inspiration for this book came in good part from an article that appeared in the March 1995 issue of NATIONAL GEOGRAPHIC: "Dead or Alive: The Endangered Species Act." I would like to thank Senior Assistant Editor John G. Mitchell, Associate Editor Robert M. Poole, Cathryn P. Buchanan, formerly of Planning Council Research, and former Editor of the Magazine, William Graves for their guidance and encouragement. Having spent several years conducting field research for the article and this book, I find that there are simply too many people to acknowledge individually for their assistance. I can only express my gratitude that folks from all walks of life were so willing to help, regardless of their particular stance on environmental issues. Finally, thanks to Joel Sartore. His ideals sparked this book, and his talents and commitment saw it through to reality.

JS: I would like to thank four people at the National Geographic Society who were critical to this project's completion: Bill Allen, for backing it from the beginning; Dennis Dimick, whose vision and picture editing skills have been steering this body of work down the right path for years; Kevin Mulroy, for coaxing all of us along; and Bill Marr, who volunteered his time and kept the faith through thick and thin to produce an outstanding design that I am very proud of.

Also contributing greatly to this book were: Steve Ahlstedt, Archbold Biological Station, Sue Behrns, Leah Bendavid-Val, Richard Biggins, Tom Boyd, Janet Brooks, Don Caulkins, Stella Cha, David Clendenen, Inez Conner, Catherine Dees, Natalie Fobes, Mike Forsberg, Mike Fritz, Betsy Hancock, Deborah Jones, Tom Kennedy, Ted Kirk, Rodger Knaggs, Dave Ledig, Cindy Lewis, Lighthawk, Mathias Botanical Garden, Rudi Mattoni, the Nature Conservancy, Mike Peters, B. "Moose" Peterson, Connie Phelps, Margaret Puckette, Red Wolf Recovery Team, Larry Richardson, Rick Rickman, David Rimlinger, David St. George, San Diego Wild Animal Park, Sea World of San Diego, Kathleen Sartore, Charlie Saylor, Steve Sherrod, Joe Stancampiano, Don Sterner, Gary Stolz, Jon Thaxton, Tom Thorne, Rebecca Yahr, Kenji Yamaguchi, U.S. Fish and Wildlife Service, Gary Zahm.

CONSULTANTS FOR ENDANGERED SPECIES ARTWORK:
Bruce Batten, Robert Bowker, Ken Burton, Steve Chambers, Spence Conley, Ann Cully, Elsie Davis, Karen Day, Susan Dreiband, Dr. David Etnier, Melinda Finger, Judy Gibson, James Godwin, Jean Harrison, Dr. Robert Hershler, Jeff Humphrey, Scott Johnson, David Klinger, Dr. Deborah Krause, Ronald Lambertson, Charlie McDonald, David Martin, Dr. Scott Miller, Ralph Morgenweck, Marge Nelson, Dr. Ronald M. Nowak, Barbara Orisich, Charles Painter, Georgia Parham, James Pulliam, Jr., John Rogers, Jr., Sharon Rose, Dr. Alan Rutberg, Connie Rutherford, Fran Scheele, Robin Shannon, Mike Smith, Dr. George Staples, Hans Stuart, David P. Tibor, Hillary Vinson, Dr. Warren Wagner, Dr. George Watson, Chris Williams, Jerri Williams, Dr. Nina Young, Dr. George R. Zug

ABOUT THE AUTHORS

Douglas H. Chadwick is a wildlife biologist. A frequent contributor to NATIONAL GEOGRAPHIC, he has written about endangered species and conservation in habitats from the Congo to the Arctic. His books include *The Fate of the Elephant*, *The Kingdom*, and National Geographic's *Enduring America*, a portrait of our nation's wild places and creatures.

Joel Sartore, a photojournalist, is a Husker through and through. He grew up in the town of Ralston, Nebraska, and later attended the University of Nebraska at Lincoln. He has been a contract photographer for NATIONAL GEOGRAPHIC since 1992 and has covered the American West extensively, focusing on land-use issues, ecosystems, and endangered species.

THE COMPANY WE KEEP America's Endangered Species
by Douglas H. Chadwick and Joel Sartore

PUBLISHED BY THE NATIONAL GEOGRAPHIC SOCIETY

Reg Murphy	*President and Chief Executive Officer*
Gilbert M. Grosvenor	*Chairman of the Board*
Nina D. Hoffman	*Senior Vice President*

PREPARED BY THE BOOK DIVISION

William R. Gray	*Vice President and Director*
Charles Kogod	*Assistant Director*
Barbara A. Payne	*Editorial Director*

STAFF FOR THIS BOOK

Kevin Mulroy	*Editor*
Bill Marr	*Art Director*
Dennis R. Dimick	*Picture Editor*
Leah Bendavid-Val	*Contributing Editor*
Mark Galan	*Researcher*
Anne E. Withers	*Contributing Researcher*
William Pitzer	*Illustrator*
David W. Wooddell	*Illustrations Researcher*
Carl Mehler	*Map Editor*
Tracey M. Wood	*Map Researcher*
Lisa R. Ritter	*Satellite Image Consultant*
Gary A. Soucie	*Picture Legends Writer*
Martha C. Christian	*Consulting Editor*
Anne Marie Houppert	*Indexer*
Jennifer L. Burke	*Illustrations Assistant*
Kevin G. Craig	*Editorial Assistant*
Richard S. Wain	*Production Project Manager*
Peggy J. Purdy	*Staff Assistant*

MANUFACTURING AND QUALITY MANAGEMENT

George V. White	*Director*
John T. Dunn	*Associate Director*
Vincent P. Ryan	*Manager*

A SUCCESS STORY A full recovery is expected for the bald eagle, whose numbers have soared as a result of the ban on DDT, captive breeding, and relocation programs. There are now believed to be over 5,000 nesting pairs of bald eagles in the lower 48 states.

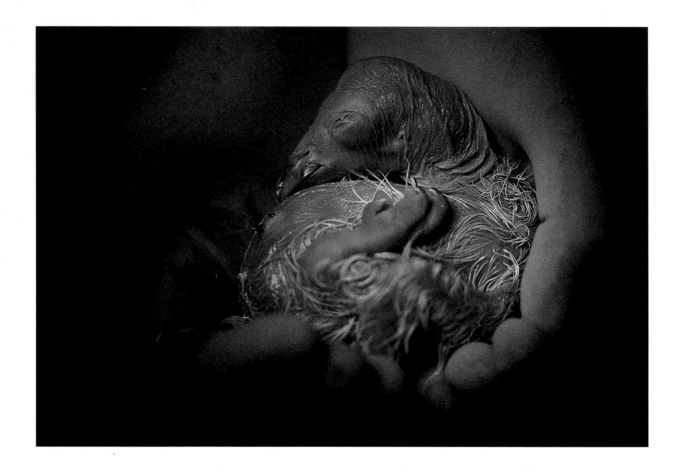

CALIFORNIA CONDOR CHICK
A newly hatched condor sleeps in the hands of a biologist at the San Diego Wild Animal Park.